COLLABORATIONS

WHERE THE WHOLE IS GREATER THAN THE SUM OF ITS PARTS

Book 3 of the
Successful Indie Author
series

by
Craig Martelle

ISBN: 9781698445663

Editing services provided by Lynne Stiegler
Cover by Sapphire Designs
Formatting (both eBook and paperback) by Drew Avera

This is a book on writing books. If that wasn't your desire in buying this eBook, then please return it within seven days for a full refund from Amazon.

INTRODUCTION

Who am I to give advice on collaborations in regard to your author career? I have more than three million words in publication, four million when you include my collaboration work (the words someone else wrote in our shared books).

But what is a collaboration? It's when two or more authors combine forces to create a single work, whether it is co-writing a story or coordinating on the story's publication. It is two or more authors bringing a story from concept to market—simple as that. It also has incredible challenges, all of which I hope to address in this book to help you make the most of your collaborations, to get them right from the outset, and to realize new levels of success in your self-published author business.

I've collaborated with a dozen different authors across a broad spectrum of titles and genres. The rewards can be substantial. The drawbacks can also be significant if you don't go into it with eyes wide open, focused on what you hope to get out of it. I want this book to bring those concerns to light.

Collaborations can be a phenomenal dynamic where the whole is greater than the sum of its parts, or it can be your worst nightmare. My intent is that this book helps you ask the right questions, set better expectations, create winning conditions, and form a writing team that delivers for readers in a way that will vault your collaboration to new and higher levels of success.

Good luck. You are about to embark on one of the best ways to grow, either your business or your personal author style. ***See the possibilities, and make great things happen.***

Roll up your sleeves, because it's time to get to work.

1

WHY COLLABORATE?

- **Business Reasons**
- **Personal Growth**
- **Fun**

There are many reasons to collaborate, and no matter what your reason, you have to establish a sound foundation.

Make sure you know which one you are embracing. One of the most destructive elements in any contractual arrangement is not having shared expectations. When two people expect the same things, the chance that you'll achieve them is far greater. If you have different expectations, you may find yourself working at cross purposes, and ultimately be dissatisfied to the point of dissolving your collaboration. That is a monumental waste of time.

Always use a contract to protect everyone involved, including your heirs. I don't often talk to collaborators. I probably should do so a bit more, but I am better with communicating through the written word. A vocal agreement is often misinterpreted or not remembered completely. What I say may not be what you heard. It's not the same for a written contract. Write it down, then conquer the world. You have a plan. Check out the Appendices, where I provide a variety of contracts for different circumstances.

Moving on to the question of why you might wish to collaborate. I see three main reasons for collaborating: business purposes, personal growth, or simple fun. Each reason can transcend and become more than originally intended. We hope that's the case, and managing the expectations at the outset is important for all parties to keep the collaboration a safe place to work and achieve at least that initial objective.

Business Reasons

The bottom line is generating more revenue, and that is what most collaborations are about, whether through direct or indirect means. Direct means each author gets a cut of something they would not have had before, and their combined efforts deliver a higher return than either would have been able to accomplish on their own (either through quicker ability to publish or through a wider offering). Indirect revenue generation is through quality exposure, maybe newsletter list growth, all while earning money.

Which is a good point to make and reinforce. A collaboration doesn't mean you write something for someone else for free purely to get exposure while the other makes money. Make sure the terms are clear, the workload is acceptable, and the desired end result is clearly spelled out.

Direct business reasons (increase revenue):

- More books with less effort
- Books a primary author has no time to write, but where the reader demand is there
- Possibly better books than what the author is capable of on his/her own
- Expand into previously unavailable markets/genres
- Grow the business
- Add horsepower

Indirect business reasons

- Focus on each author's strengths
- The unspoken exposure (there, I said it)—but exposure in a good way, with an intentional business result.

No one does everything well. Some write well. Some market well. Some connect with the readers well. How do we get the most from our strengths, while minimizing our weaknesses? Collaborate. What if there is a gap in what you are offering your rabid fans? You need to fill it, but you don't have time to write all the words.

For example, an individual who has had a successful career wants to grow their offering. An established author may search for a collaborator to help him/her add books to the backlist.

What about an individual who writes well, but can never seem to find an audience? That good author could benefit from a collaborative arrangement with someone who is good at marketing, or maybe even a marketing genius who has trouble writing a gripping tale.

These collaborations come down to time versus effort. I firmly believe that anything can be learned, but some things take a great deal more effort than others. A collaborator can help an author fill a gap quickly. In other words, work smarter, not harder, to achieve your business goals.

The business factor for collaborating is all about bringing in more revenue, either now or later. Collaborate for a share of future profits. Collaborate to offset a self-publishing weakness (the writing or the marketing).

Add horsepower to your business. A recent example of this was K.F. Breene pairing up with Shannon Mayer to write the *Shadowspell Academy* series. This (Urban Fantasy set in a school with young adults) is a hot genre as of the writing of this book. Those two delivered three books that were still ranked in the five hundreds four months after publication. Between them and their well-established audiences, their collaborative books rocketed up the charts. They tapped their individual audiences, and with great sales came more exposure for all their books. Amazon likes winners and helps promote the books that sell well. When extremely talented and successful authors combine their efforts, the results can be eye-popping. I suspect that series has made them excellent money, as well as brought new readers to their backlists, which is a double win for two authors who were doing just fine on their own. But they knew they could do a little better and showed the rest of us what that looked like.

In science fiction, we have the *Dune* books that came after Frank Herbert passed away. His son Brian picked up the torch and collaborated with Kevin J. Anderson to deliver a knock-out set of books with long legs and great staying power. The worlds will live on, thanks to two great authors hammering out a better book together than they could have done alone.

Collaborations can grow individual brands and strengthen bottom lines.

It's nice to make more money. It's better when you can do that in less time. For the established author, collaborating in any kind of 50/50 (or variation) arrangement means you can add a new title in half the time, and potentially with half the work (or less). Growing one's backlist can mean an increase in visibility and business viability. Partnering with a bigger-name author can improve your visibility if your writing is already sound. That being said, I don't recommend approaching big names with offers to collaborate if they haven't asked for people to contact them or you don't already have an existing relationship.

How much work does each party need to do? That's up for grabs in the negotiation, based on your individual strengths. Maybe the relationship is 70/30—70% for the one who wrote the great story, as long as the up-front costs (cover & editing) are recovered first. Work effort, risk, and potential earnings are all important points to consider. I'll discuss these later.

I do not recommend collaborations that are purely mercenary (make money at the expense of ethics and common decency). If you're willing to trample someone to make money, maybe you should return this book. I'm a fan of the rising tide, and that we can all win together. Making money is important because it allows us to keep doing what we do but making money at all costs is a hard way to live your life. So don't do it. Look at a business relationship that will be financially beneficial to all parties involved. I hope it becomes a long-term relationship, but if you go your separate ways after the contract terms have been met, that's fine, too.

Be upright in all you do. That will sometimes mean you have to cut ties. You may find out after the process has started that you are not compatible. This is when the out-clause in your contract will come in handy. Better to cut ties early than continue a painful existence. Don't let it destroy you. Better to move on.

Thich Nhat Hanh said, "When you plant lettuce, if it does not grow well, you

don't blame the lettuce. You look for reasons it is not doing well. It may need fertilizer, or more water, or less sun. You never blame the lettuce. Yet if we have problems with our friends or family, we blame the other person. But if we know how to take care of them, they will grow well, like the lettuce. Blaming has no positive effect at all, nor does trying to persuade using reason and argument. That is my experience. No blame, no reasoning, no argument, just understanding."

The way to get to that level of nirvana is to make sure your expectations of each other and the final product are crystal-clear at the outset. ***Take a shared journey on a mutually agreed-to path. It makes things much easier.***

Personal Growth

Getting better at what we do is important. Is a profession where you're perfect without practice is worth having? I doubt such a profession exists. Keep in mind that there is no such thing as perfect. The readers decide if they like it or not, then vote with their money to buy the next book.

Even the greats practice. Prince, considered the best guitarist by people like Eric Clapton, always practiced. Top athletes have coaches. And top authors write and then write some more. They get feedback from trusted sources, and they write the next book a little better.

In a mentor/mentee situation, one helps the other grow through guidance and feedback. The mentee does the majority of the heavy lifting, but that is in exchange for the learning. Some people pay big money to be mentored. What if your only investment was time and a willingness to learn?

I've seen one representation of the learning cycle as See, Do, Teach, teaching being the element that helps one master their art. When the student becomes the teacher, the cycle has gone full circle until the next challenge and a new cycle of See, Do, Teach begins. Who learns more, the student or the teacher? Once you've become the teacher, you'll discover that both learn a great deal through the process.

How do collaborations help your personal growth? Collaborators of like minds who are friends become closer because of building something together. Remember working on a class project with one of your parents? I'm not talking about the one you waited until the night before to tell them about, but one that you planned, spent countless hours putting together, and cheered when it worked like it was supposed to. Those are the memories that last forever. Those moments are what make life worth living.

Every book could be that way, too. writing a book is unlike

most people's regular job. It's the best job in the world, telling stories to readers. And they pay you for it. Collaborations can make us bigger, better, faster, and all the other good things, if managed from the beginning and done for reasons that you both agree to.

Fun

When authors of comparable ability and or marketing prowess get together, they can be peers and partners in the creation process, sharing ideas and encouraging each other to be better. The process becomes a friendly competition to spur each other to greater heights.

They have an idea and throw it together. It leads to great things. Think of the comedy duos out there—Bing Crosby and Danny Kaye, Laurel and Hardy, Abbot and Costello, Key and Peele, Penn and Teller. Sometimes, great minds feed off each other in a way that nourishes the soul.

Look at yourself in the mirror of a partner's face. A knowing smile. A twitch. A thought turned to words becoming a catalyst for a plot. The world around it takes shape, gets painted in. It's you and someone just like you creating something wonderful.

Collaborators get to do fun things. You both write the story, and the story dominates. Maybe you'll make a little money, too. That makes it even more fun, but that wasn't the initial motivation. Fun collaborations are about having fun first and foremost. Enjoy the process of telling a story. Leverage each other's strengths. Enjoy the moment.

Even fun collaborations need a contract since sometimes a

fun project can make a lot of money. Write up a contract before or after, but make sure you have one. Stay friends and stay friendly.

And don't forget...

Have fun.

2

SELECTING A COLLABORATOR

- **How do you make sure you're collaboration material?**
- **Types of relationships**
- **Based on need**
- **Based on quality**
- **Where to look**
- **What to look for in a collaborator**
- **A collaborator portfolio**

Finding the right collaborator is critical for your mental health. Working with the wrong collaborator can be soul-sucking and costly. Be patient and watch with a critical eye.

The right person could take two minutes to find, or two years. And just like love, you'll know it when you see it, but you have to get past the first infatuation stage to find the real person beyond. Crisis shows you the true nature of the individual. Adversity is the window into the soul. How will your collaborator hold up if there's an issue that creeps into their life?

Life happens. Do you respond or react? One requires a pause, some input, and a lot of communication. The other is more immediate and less productive. I've had collaborators disappear for months at a time. It's a bit unnerving. And I don't know what to do to weed out folks who will self-destruct on you other than start slow by asking for samples of 5k-word sections, then get to 20k to see how the process went. Were there any red flags? Don't ignore them. Get a reasonable explanation or move on. Remember, when you start on a series, you make a promise to your readers. You will have to deliver even if your collaborator is long gone.

Why would I make it sound like collaborating can be a horror show? Because there is a certain risk in everything you do. Finding the perfect collaborator is an extremely rewarding experience when done right with the right people. It takes thorough screening, hard questions, and good answers, and most importantly, building trust. And there is only one way to do that.

Do what you say you're going to do.

I have a great wealth of experience in picking collaborators who didn't work out. I wanted to help them, but at the end, they were draining my energy at a fantastic rate. I was on the losing end of risk versus reward. I don't want you to go through what I have gone through. Learn from my experience! Be wise at my expense.

Set the stage well, choose your actors wisely, and you shall be rewarded with a great show.

This section is about selecting a collaborator. Once you

decide to collaborate, take the next step to determine what type of collaboration works best, then go to workload, and finally to the contract.

Let's get to it. How do we avoid the pain and suffering of a failed collaboration?

How do you make sure you're collaboration material?

Be who you are, or become who you want to be. Does that sound mysterious enough? Make promises you can reasonably fulfill. Under-promise and over-deliver. Make sure you gave yourself plenty of time, especially if you're new. Ask questions early and often, not late, and hardly at all. Have a portfolio of your writing style. If you have never finished a book, do not be surprised if someone is skeptical about co-writing with you.

The even easier answer is to make sure you finish the first book. And then finish another one. Showing your ability to get it done on time is important.

Collaborations are about having an eye on a goal. Writing for writing's sake is neat, but that's a hobby. I'm talking about a viable product you can sell. To do that, it has to be complete. It helps if it's a great story or a good story told in a great way.

Questions you need to ask yourself (and you have to be honest):

- Why do I want to collaborate?
- How far am I willing to compromise?
- Will this help me improve my writing? What if it doesn't?

- Will this help me improve the business side?
- What amount of time am I willing & able to commit? When will I work on my personal books?
- How many words can I reasonably write in a week, no matter what else happens in my life?
- Will I be able to make changes/rewrite sections quickly in order to maintain momentum?
- Will I be available for conversations (phone or text) within a reasonable response time (a day or less, unless you've coordinated ahead of time)?
- What secrets must I keep regarding our collaboration?
- Most important, will I meet my commitments?

I include these questions as the bellwether of a collaboration. Being ghosted is a horrendous experience. A book is due, and the co-author is MIA (missing in action). This usually happens later in the series, toward the end, when the author has mentally moved on to the next project. But you owe it to your readers, the ones who are still committed to the series, to finish it, so finish it you must. My friend Martha Carr finished writing a book while sitting next to her sister's deathbed. Why? Because the collaborator ghosted her.

If you commit to it, meet your commitment. That is the foundation of all business transactions. No contract language will get a book written by someone who doesn't want to write it. It's important to stay in touch, keep everything aboveboard, and by all that's holy, keep your promises!

If you can't do that, you are not long-term collaborator material. Maybe a standalone collaboration has a greater potential for success. I've done these, and they are far better for all parties in the collaboration relationship. With a single book, it's easier to work through issues and get the book finished and published. With an eight-book story arc, small issues can become big ones.

Learn what it's like to be a collaborator. For those of you who are married, it's exactly like that, without the warm and fuzzies. It's better to ease into it than jump across the threshold and slam the door behind you. Go on a few dates first. Take care of small issues before committing long-term.

I guarantee you'll have an initial period of great excitement and energy. Capture some words and start sharing. Get to the grind, and see how well it still works. You might surprise yourself with a newfound ability. Having accountability could be the catalyst you need, but someone has to take a chance on you first. Do you need someone cracking a whip over your head, or can you succeed by cracking it yourself?

But here we are after the excitement has waned and you're tired, or the other parts of your life are eating up space. This is when you may need to dig in and decide how badly you want it. Either way, staying engaged is the best thing you can do to maintain a smooth and productive conversation, and that means not disappearing from contact.

If you're going offline for a week, that's fine. Just make sure your collaborator knows when you'll be back. It is important not to disappear. This may sound like common sense, but it is not. Ghosting someone, even unintentionally, will forever leave a bad taste. That being said, make sure you have multiple ways to contact each other, like phone, email, and messenger. At least three ways, just in case your phone gets stolen and you change numbers. In case you get booted from Facebook for a rules violation. Have a backup since your collaborator will only see that you're gone and not know why.

Can you get the work done? Don't be starry-eyed and sign up for something you aren't capable of writing. If Diana Gabaldon asked me to co-author an epic romance story with her, I couldn't do it. I would have to turn her down because I know that I'm not going to do the research necessary in that genre to do it right. Practice honesty in all things, and most importantly, be honest with yourself. Maybe you can learn to write something else, but make sure your collaborator knows you're going through OJT (on-the-job training), so delivery at the beginning might be slower because there are more questions.

Questions are good. They forestall issues. Answering the same question multiple times? Not so good. Again, you have to gauge the small issues to assess how the collaboration is going. Stay in touch, and stay on top of things.

I added the question above regarding secrets. Everyone has secrets. Can you keep your collaborator's? This goes back to trust. As your relationship grows, you might learn things like their real name. You might learn they have other pen names. They might talk about upcoming projects that aren't meant to be public. These are secrets you need to keep. I know a few romance authors who also have erotica pen names. They don't tell anyone because they are two wildly different markets. No one needs to know.

Meeting your commitments will make all things easier. Missing delivery dates and/or not rolling up expected word counts aren't good. Once you start making excuses, it gets easier to make more excuses. Do what you say you're going to do, and sometimes that might mean saying "No." If your collaborator asks you for an extra story, whether a full-length novel or just a novelette, but you don't have time, be upright. Tell your collaborator that you can't do it, or inform them of the timeframe to get it done.

Don't let expectations linger. Don't over-commit. Under-promise and over-deliver.

Here's a secret: more people have bad co-authoring experiences than good. These questions, and this whole book, is about how to improve your chances to have a good experience.

Types of relationships

Are you or can you be friends? It's a simple test, but an important one. Do you get along? If something about the other person grates on your soul, you probably won't be able to overlook it once a deadline is missed. Note the cues.

What do you like? What don't you like? Will the person respond amicably if you mention something the collaborator is doing that you might not be completely comfortable with? And most importantly, can you live with everything you're hearing?

Be honest with yourself. If the answers to those questions are yes, chalk it up as a win. Leverage each other's strengths for a partnership that will withstand the test of time.

Do you have mutual respect? I would hope so. Why would I want to bring on a co-author I don't respect? Why would you want to work with someone you can't take seriously? That's prostitution-level work. There are better ways to earn money, or at least ways where you don't feel dirty at the end.

Mutual respect and friendship. Those are good ways to start the conversation regarding a collaboration. Compromise and understanding. Eyes on the prize, which is, keep your focus on the goal while dealing with the details en route.

Another relationship is a shared business interest. It's not getting in bed with the enemy, but it *is* leveraging your combined strengths to access a market that neither of you could tap alone. You already know each other, and offer to collaborate for a singular purpose.

What if you don't know your potential collaborator? I suggest you get to know them before you go too far. Can you get references from trusted sources? Don't get married before the first date, no matter how gorgeous they seem. That's only a façade. You're collaborating with the person behind the curtain. Go back there and take a look. Then decide if you can do business.

- Business
- Friendship
- Mutual respect

Business, friendship, or mutual respect. Those are the three relationships with the greatest chance of success. You'll see that I didn't list "desperation." This goes back to being honest with yourself. If you have to keep compromising, the situation is not right for you. If you find yourself saying, "I'll take anything," you are not in the best position to negotiate. You're giving the other person carte blanche to take advantage of you, and you will quickly sour on the relationship. You'll feel worse than when you started, and it will have cost you time, money, and maybe even some of your hair.

Desperation is not a good foundation for any relationship. Even if you are desperate, be discriminating in the relationships you form. The good ones will float to the top.

Based on need

The desperation part was my segue into a collaboration based on need. Both (or all) collaborators have a need to fill, whether it's more words, a story that an established readership wants to see, revenue, and a myriad of other reasons. A need for a book is there and must be filled!

Thus begins the search. Having your need clearly defined makes it easier. That was what Michael Anderle had when he approached me in the fall of 2016. He had a side story in his universe he had no intention of writing. I'm including his email to me on that fateful day...

From Michael Anderle
Wed 10/12/2016 7:53 AM
To Craig Martelle, Author

Craig,

In books 12 and 13, I have a character (ex-military, mercenary - good-ish guy) that I'm thinking is going to stay on Earth instead of going with team(s) due to relationship with a Professor that is also in the stories.

. . .

If you are willing, we can talk about whether he is a good character to use for your series as some fans are wanting to know what happens with him. My thought, if you concur, is to juice him up a little for his support of TQB which would allow him to last through the time (spruce him back up and give him enough that he should 'last' to 120 - same with her ...But, she will die of course) ... Plus, Akio would know him (or at least remember him).

He has a certain level of 'what's in it for me' attitude that would fit our story discussions last week.

Not sure how to go from here on the idea... I can pull his chapters, maybe? Or just download books 12 and 13 and look for 'Terry' (the guy) and read those sections?

Michael.

There it is. The complete offer. I did not accept right away. It took a couple of phone calls and me reading those referenced books. The ex-military? A Marine (and there are no ex-Marines, only former Marines because Once a Marine, Always a Marine). I might be biased).

Michael knew what he was asking for but gave me the

latitude to flesh out the character. I didn't write the Marine as Michael had, but for the fans, that didn't matter as much as how the story was told. They embraced my style for this series. And that is what was great about working with Michael. I didn't have to replicate his style. He is a big fan of the story first. Create characters the readers care about and take them on a great journey.

We did all that. Michael had a need. And then we became friends, and then close friends. He's one of the few people I would hop on a plane for today. All he has to do is ask. All because of a collaborative relationship that started with a need. We had known each other before we started to collaborate, so we understood our respective work ethics. He knew I would jam tirelessly to get the words, tell the story, and continue to the next. I delivered on my promises. I stayed in touch. And we delivered a winner to the fans.

A need-based relationship could also describe an employer/employee arrangement, which is exactly what a work-for-hire or ghostwriter collaboration is. The need is there. The relationship might be less personal, but it doesn't need to be.

For a ghostwriter, some people go through an agency, and the ghost isn't supposed to know who they are writing for. It would not be hard to find out once the book is published, but that's beside the point. In those instances, the ghosts generally sign non-disclosure agreements to maintain secrecy and the identity of the author.

I personally don't use ghostwriters, but there's many an author who got their start that way. Some prefer to work that way, at least for a while, to know how much money they'll be receiving and be sure they can pay their bills. Nothing wrong with that. They learned to meet deadlines, hit word counts, flex to the employer's needs, and adjust their writing style as necessary. They learned some critical self-publishing skills while getting paid for the lessons. The ghostwriters are able to work from home, which is a big bonus to many. Money when you need it is a great deal, especially when you've earned it. Someone took a risk on you, just like any other day job you were hired for. Someone thought you would help them earn more than you cost them.

This can be a pure employer/employee relationship. It's about the pay, but it's a lesson in life. How many people left their day jobs to start their own business in the same line of work? Same thing here. Or how about a hybrid arrangement—less money per word, but a share of the royalties?

If you're paying the ghostwriter, this is a great option once you've worked with the writer on a few books and know you have a winning relationship. You grow into a different arrangement. The hybrid option is a business deal that is gaining traction. It's like joining an employee-owned business, which modifies the employer/employee relationship rather significantly. The ghostwriter is now personally invested in the success of the book. If you're the ghostwriter, better to be an owner-operator unless you're on the side that needs as much money as you can get *now*. Sometimes, a bird in hand is worth more than two in the bush.

But know why you as the ghostwriter are making the decision to put yourself into the relationship. What's the least amount you can afford to make now to have a longer-term interest? And what if you show so much potential that the employer, the bigger name author, brings you on in a different collaboration role? What kind of value does that have? What are you willing to do if you're the employer?

Can you see the potential when you take off your artist hat and put on your business hat? Knowing your why is critical to making decisions that are in your best financial interests.

There will be no surprises in the resulting relationship. In business, surprises are usually a bad thing, so eliminate them when you can, or at least reduce them greatly.

Collaborations based on need start in a less personal manner but can grow into something a lot more, or you simply cut ties at the end and each go your merry way once the need has been filled.

Based on quality

Trying to collaborate if you have no portfolio is a great challenge. What I mean by this is that you don't have proof of your writing chops and your skills and abilities to bounce off a potential collaborator's strengths and weaknesses. There's no way to know if you're a good fit. You have to have something.

A quality collaboration is an arrangement where each collaborator fills a writing gap the other has. Dialogue. Plot. Characters. Whatever it might be, the overall quality grows when the two complement each other.

"Nice plot!"

"Thank you. Exceptional dialogue!"

Sorry, not that kind of compliment. If you have a shortcoming in quality, you might look for a collaborator to help you grow. You're good, but maybe not good enough. Or maybe you want to be great. The two can build a better story together.

These types of collaborations are mutually beneficial, and they could be put into any of the arrangements you see in the next chapter.

This is a short sub-section, but I wanted to make sure you could collaborate rather than hire a book coach or a developmental editor. Can you do it yourself, and are you willing to learn? Once you start studying plot development (I recommend the MasterClass series of videos), you might find you get it.

If you can do it yourself, then do it, since you'll retain 100% of your earnings. Knowing how to write a complete story and sell it is important. It lets you ask smarter questions when you collaborate, for a more meaningful engagement. Think of the possibilities. Collaborating doesn't mean you can wipe your hands of that part of the collaboration. Don't be the anchor that holds your partnership back.

For reference, a book coach is much like a mentor but is someone who is paid to walk you through various aspects. Whereas a mentor helps out of mutual respect and personal gratification, a book coach is less emotionally invested. Developmental editors have a tendency to be very expensive. They talk high-level plot issues, dissecting your storyline and rebuilding it, with you to improve the overall story. I've never used one or a book coach, so I can't talk about the value of their services. I can talk about doing it all yourself.

Although I've collaborated a fair bit, I have a huge number of titles that were all me. I think it's important to be able to walk the walk. How can you give guidance to others if you haven't done it yourself? I remain skeptical of indie self-help gurus who have published one book.

You can learn as you create a sellable product, and it's important to always be learning in this business. The book business is constantly changing and evolving. Don't be behind the power curve. That is for players who aren't willing or able to flex to change. Sometimes that takes a willingness to say "I don't know" and then listen more than you speak. Indies are in the best position to adapt to industry changes and profit off being able to meet the new demands more quickly.

The whole is greater than the sum of the parts. Think about where you've lost stars in your reviews. What if a collaborator helped write those parts, and you helped write what he/she wasn't great at? Adapting. Overcoming challenges. Staying at the front of the industry.

That's where a quality-based relationship blossoms, and like the others, it can expand into a real friendship, even if you both go your separate ways after your collaboration has run its course. We always remember those who helped us when we were in need.

Where do you find potential collaborators?

This is the big question most people have. Here are some places to look and how to look, but ingenuity can be your friend. Think about where you might meet a person who keeps mostly to themselves. That's the challenge, so you have to find them when they appear in public, either online (most have a presence) or in person (there have been rare sightings).

- **Online**

- **Social Media – Facebook/Twitter/Instagram/Reddit/etc.**
- **Blogs**
- **Amazon – Look Inside their books or read their books**
- **Participation in anthologies, group box sets**
- **In person**
- **Conferences**
- **Local writing groups**
- **Conventions (DragonCon, ComiCon, things like those)**
- **Coffee shops and elsewhere**

Online

By running the author Facebook group *20Booksto50k®*, I am in a unique position to find people, but we've opened up a co-author as well as ghostwriter thread that can help expedite the process. Look there for people who write in your genre and then do your research. Have they written a book, and how does it read? Well enough, or better than what you can do? Be able to answer why when they ask what's in it for them besides the curse word "exposure" or potential profit.

"You write the book, and we'll split the profits." That is a horrible offer, and one that most authors receive from their friends who think they have a good idea for a book but have no idea what it takes. I return to my point about writing a book. Co-authoring with someone who has never written a book is a high-risk proposition.

I don't recommend you do it.

How do you maintain your social media presence, no matter which platform you use? This is your brand. This is where you tout that obscure genre that dominates or the big genre you enjoy. Remember, genre = marketing. Your brand should fully support what will sell you the most books to the readers who will love them, and you can expand from there. It will also help you find someone with comparable chops, that is, with a comparable style, dedication, work ethic, and genre.

On Facebook, I never meant for my personal page to be my public page, but it happened. I don't post anything political or religious. I shy away from memes because I have no idea who is where. I have some 3000 followers on my personal page, and 1500 on my author page, which is a public page. It's okay. I post stuff to both places, and my brand is solid. I'm sure I have posts from four or five years ago that if someone digs deeply enough, they might find something I said once and be offended. I can't help that. I don't have the time to go back, and I didn't know my brand then, but I know it now. That's what people see. That is my public face, and I also think it represents my private self, too. That's the best path to take, being authentic, and when you can find a collaborator who operates on the same wavelength, you have the start of something.

I share a lot about books because they are important to me. I'm an author. Of course, I care about the written word. But which words, and how are they strung together? That's where we try to impress the followers. I will edit my posts if something isn't clear or there's a typo. I never know who may be looking.

People will judge you. If your posts are incomprehensible, a potential reader might shy away. In my book *Write Compelling Fiction*, Larry and I emphasize the point that you should never give a reader a reason to put your book down. Don't give them a reason not to pick it up in the first place!

That's the power (and the risk) of social media, but that one place you might find readers or collaborators. I do a lot of business online. A lot. Stay on brand, and you'll be amazed at what comes your way.

Build a portfolio you can share, even if you've written a hundred books. What is your best work that you are proud to share? Is that what you aspire to improve upon? Is that the standard to which you'll hold a co-author?

If you're the potential collaborator, you'll want to aspire to that, too. Are you close enough to do it? I once wanted to write a *Dragonriders of Pern* book, but upon re-reading the first three, I would have to labor too hard over each sentence. I do some of the things well, but other terms she uses and her overall language are outside the way I think. It would be extremely frustrating for me to try to write a whole book that way. As flattering as an offer to do such a book would be, I have to be realistic. You should, too.

Being honest with yourself is the best way to establish shared expectations you'll be happy to meet. It's that fun thing again, and frankly, even in a relationship to make money, if all the fun is drained out of it, why do it? So where does this take us?

Back to finding collaborators. I'm talking an online search. Have you found some books that aren't selling well but you love how they're written? That could be an author open to collaborating. Such authors might disappear if they aren't nurtured (book sales are dismal). Reach out and see. They'll have contact information somewhere. If not, they're not open to communication, so move on.

The search for a collaborator is through their stories. If you start with what you read, you might be able to find a partner.

How about on their Facebook page (personal or author), where they share their word counts and snippets of their story?

I'm not sure I would ever find a collaborator on Twitter since I can't comprehend most of the coolest tweets. I find myself at a hashtag loss, but if you click with someone there, why not see what else drives them?

Check out their author blogs and read what they share with their fans.

Look at what books they have published using the Amazon Look Inside feature, where you can review a great deal of work at no cost. I'm a big fan of setting the hook in the first five hundred words. Look Inside and see what there is to see.

I publish a science fiction anthology once or twice a year with twenty to thirty short stories. The submissions show me a person's writing style and ability to follow direction. I require a certain font, size, and spacing, solely to gauge the level of professionalism of the submitting author. I've found that the most established will always submit according to my direction. Those who are up and coming can follow direction, too. Authors who run on pure emotion have a tendency to press Send before checking the details of the submission, focusing exclusively on their story to carry the day.

I run a business, so to me, the details are important. So is a great story. I want both. Those who can do both usually are the cream of the crop, even if they're new. Those who miss the details? I still read their stories, but they are carrying two strikes. I've found that most of those stories have fatal flaws. Details. They are what lifts a hobby author to the status of a seasoned professional. Collaborators want no less.

When you collaborate, it's important to get the small details correct. It sets the stage for the more important issues.

And that's what I look for in collaborators. I expect I'm not the only one. I've tried collaborating with people who run on pure emotion. It was tragic for my blood pressure. It's like trying to get your Jack Russell Terrier to relax so you can watch a movie while a road crew is working in front of your house. There is emotion that goes into every story. I think they'd be crap without connecting to readers on an emotional level. But you have to keep that out of your business life. Making business decisions in an emotional state don't work out for the best. Lock the doors and take a break. You'll be better for it.

And so will your collaborator. Shared expectations. It's a business, but it's art. You can revel in the joy of creation without getting lost in the high. Would you find your optimal collaborator at Woodstock on a week-long high? Probably not. But you might find him/her at a coffee shop getting those words, reworking a scene until it was perfect.

In person

Writers' conferences are another source for collaborators. When people meet, sometimes they click. Those are the relationships that are good foundations for creating a great story.

Even the most introverted among us can find a writing soulmate.

I have to tout the 20Books conferences. We've had them around the world, in Vegas (our flagship show), London, Edinburgh, Adelaide, and Bali. Lifelong friendships are made at these shows. We set up Facebook groups so attendees can get glimpses of each other in a way that's safe for all. A couple of comments later, and they're sitting next to each other in Vegas. After that, the sky is the limit.

If we never leave our homes, we might not reach that collaboration nirvana that one can achieve in person, but we can still get where we want to go.

Over the phone, Skype, Zoom, or whatever video call system is the in thing when you're reading this. See the person. Get to know them. Talk about the fun stuff and the contract stuff.

Shared expectations. It's what makes for great collaborations.

Isn't it better to talk through that stuff in person? You can assess how each is engaged with the hard stuff while generating energy from the fun conversations.

In person. At least you can have a coffee together. Unless you drink tea or soda or whisky. Then do that. Even introverts. If you've found someone who writes in your genre and you saw other things online that tickled your fancy, you'll find that you have a great deal in common. Skip the small talk and go right to the heart of it. What's your favorite witch characteristic? What's your opinion on unicorns? How much weaponry should a foot soldier of the twenty-third century carry? So many important things that need talking about. The weather is the weather.

You'll be amazed by how quickly time passes when you are engaged, talking about what matters most to you. And if you share the writing with such a person? That's a collaboration based on friendship and shared interest.

Start with one story and see where it leads you. Back to my anthology. Two guys. One short story. They now have an eleven-book contract together. Collaborations for the win. And it started with a five-thousand-word short.

Local writing groups are another way to find someone who you might be interested in writing with. Make sure you start with honesty. Sometimes a façade is important to keep your sanity, but not when you're looking for a collaborator. Your veneer will pale and shatter under the stress of writing a book.

Conventions, coffee shops, and anywhere authors hang out. Don't hunt them down, as in stalk them, but be aware. Always have your portfolio available, even if it's simply a link to your website. You never know when the right person will show up. Don't fail before you begin by not being ready. Give them a chance to like you and your work. If they don't, that's fine. Don't take it personally. But if they didn't have the opportunity to look because you didn't have a card for them, that's not setting yourself up for success.

And we always want to be ready to win. Even if you only have one card on you. That's all I carry (but I always have at least one). Use it wisely.

What to look for in a collaborator

I address all these things elsewhere, but people like lists.

Here's the too-long, didn't-read version of what to look for in a collaborator.

- Ability—do they write to your standards or better?
- Compatibility—can you get along? Can your brands?
- Trustworthiness—do they deliver on their promises?
- Work ethic—do they work as hard as you do?
- Integrity—are they honest with you?

A collaborator portfolio

I mentioned a portfolio a couple of times above, so I thought it best to explain further. That is a sample of your work. It is the standard to which you hold yourself and how you represent yourself.

- Samples of your work
- Contact information
- Samples of your thoughts (your social media presence and blog)
- Your desires

In the early days, I hated to give my work away for free. Now? I'll give someone five different short stories or an entire series if they want, but here's my trick. I'll gift it to them from Amazon. With the 70% royalty (minus download fee), it only costs me 35%, and I don't run afoul of my exclusivity agreement since most of my books are in KU. Many of my short stories are not, and I send those directly via BookFunnel. There's my portfolio—here's how I write.

My Amazon page will show that I've co-authored fifty or sixty titles. That's also my portfolio. I talk about upcoming books on my blog page and sometimes wax poetic on other stories I have in mind. More portfolio. I have a big online presence. I've worked hard to establish my brand, so I have no problem leveraging that exposure to cast a wide net when looking for a collaborator to write the next big series.

It doesn't always bear fruit because I'm a big softie. I should say "No" more quickly, but I give people a chance. For the record, this isn't an open call to spam me. I will approach folks if I have a collaboration project, or if I meet someone who gets me. You need to be prepared to say "No" if that's the right reply. You don't want to marry the wrong person (some of us are too painfully aware of that).

I have my contact information scattered everywhere. I'm not hard to get hold of. My email is on my Amazon page and my homepage. My FB profile is set to public. I do get some creepy stalker stuff, but I live so far away from the rest of the world that those people are just stupid and a waste of time. My address is a PO Box down the road. People can find multiple ways to contact me. The jury duty people have no problem finding me even though I never get selected. That's a waste of time too, but I do my duty. I show up.

Your thoughts and your desires. I'm not talking personal stuff. What is your professional goal? Do you want to be a ghostwriter, telling great stories, but no one knows who you are? Does that better meet your financial comfort level? There are people like that, and I understand their reasons. I tell them not to undervalue their work even though they can't share much of their portfolio because of non-disclosure agreements. Good words rate good pay.

Do you want to collaborate on a trilogy and then move on with your newfound knowledge? Then be upfront about that! It's grating to sign a contract for eight books and someone bails after two because they think they have it all figured out. That's not a good reputation to establish. Trust in business is a good thing. Be trustworthy, but set yourself up for success. Don't sign a contract for eight books if you think you might only do three.

That's part of your portfolio, too. Testimonials. See if you can get some. They carry a lot of weight with me. I prefer people who have some experience collaborating, even if it's not the same type of collaboration they've done before.

Their other books don't even need to have sold well. That's not a concern for me since the quality of writing and meeting commitments are what I'm looking for. And I'm not alone in that.

If you collaborate, your brand needs to remain strong since that's your portfolio. That's how you'll find more work.

Be your brand, and make it strong.

3

TYPES OF COLLABORATIONS

- **Partnership (50/50, that sort of thing)**
- **Roundtable**
- **Senior/junior**
- **Mentor/mentee**
- **Work for hire**
- **Ghostwriting**
- **Anthologies**
- **The bottom line**

There are many reasons to collaborate. Make sure you know which one you are embracing and you both agree. One of the most destructive elements in any contractual arrangement is not having shared expectations. When two people expect the same things, the chance that you'll achieve them is far greater. If you have different expectations, you might find yourself working at cross purposes, and ultimately be dissatisfied to the point of dissolving your collaboration. That is a monumental waste of time and energy.

I always encourage the use of contracts that both people have read and concur with. A contract is not something to be wielded like a club, but the common page from which people operate. The contract is the shared expectations memorialized in written form. Save yourself the grief of misremembering by having it in writing.

You don't need to use lawyer language. You simply need both (or multiple parties) to understand what everyone needs to do in the same way. Having a shared lexicon and a mutual goal is the best way to stave off any problems before they happen.

Turn yourselves loose on what you want to accomplish and make the magic happen.

Equal Partnership

When authors of comparable ability and/or marketing prowess get together, they can be co-equal partners in the creation process.

Two authors hash out the story premise and the outline, combine forces to write the story, work over each other's parts, revise, and finally come to a consensus on the final product. Through the give and take, the story becomes stronger.

Build in enough time to work through these issues. Your motivation to work together should come from mutual respect, but when you show someone your unedited draft, it's like opening the closet to your skeletons. But your co-author is going to do the same thing. By seeing how the other's engine operates, you get an in-depth look into both of your minds. The rewrite.

The tweak. The adjustments to blend one's style into the other. Become one that is stronger than the individual parts.

It takes a lot of give and take. It's also time to put your ego aside. If you are convinced your version is correct, you need to convince your co-author of the same through intellectual persuasion, possibly delivering an alternative versus letting it degenerate. I talked about shared expectations. Maybe get a trusted reader to look at the two versions and determine which hits the mark better. No matter what, someone has to be the final arbiter, and that is an important element to put into a contract.

What happens when you disagree? Who gets the work product in case you dissolve the collaboration? Would it be better to publish something you're not necessarily ecstatic about rather than let it rot, or worse, destroy it outright?

Before the words are written and the book is published, you need to know what follows. You want to know who is going to do what when it comes to advertising and marketing the final product. Who makes the ad graphics, and who arranges external promotions? Help each other manage the expectations.

In a mutual collaboration, all these things can be carried as a shared burden, make it easier for everyone. And that is the positive result of a collaboration—share the tasks to deliver something greater than either of you would be able to do by yourself.

Enough cheerleading, 50/50 doesn't necessarily mean you each write exactly the same number of words. It means that you each do fifty percent of the work. It takes me roughly eighty focused hours to write a solid 65k-word book. Maybe your collaborator then pays for the editing and the cover and coordinates the proofreaders, while also building the launch campaign and running ads. Is that equal to eighty hours of writing time?

This is what a 50/50 collaboration looks like. Parcel out the tasks until you are each carrying an equal burden. Whether it's shared time, treasure, or talent, both of you should contribute fairly to the final product—a book that sells.

This exact same logic applies to a 60/40, 70/30, 75/25, or any other kind of arrangement. Make sure that you both agree up front what the separate workloads look like. A little horse-trading could be called for, like, two hours of writing equals one hour of ads manipulation. It might be a good trade-off. The sky is the limit on what elements you can work out because now there are two of you splitting the load for all the elements. Since you're a self-published author, at least one of you should know what "all" the elements are. Write them down and throw them on the table, just like picking teams. To each of you, what is the value of each task that must be done? Negotiate. Establish the expectations and then strive to exceed them.

Roundtable

This is a unique collaboration that spread-loads the stress of publishing quickly.

Two, three, four, or more collaborators write in the same universe, telling stories that complement each other. Each collaborator writes the whole story. The group then takes turns publishing their books but under the same pen name (these are for one set of established fans).

The editing and cover process are managed as a group. One

or more of the other collaborators reads the others' stories to make sure that they adhere to canon while also growing the universe. I've seen this done successfully in Romance and Science Fiction. There's no reason it couldn't work in other genres that create new worlds for their characters.

The team of collaborators delivers a book for publication every one to two weeks, with each author having to write a book every four to six weeks. It's not overwhelming and keeps a certain readership happy. If you have 10,000 readers (a drop in the overall readership bucket) and can deliver a book a week to them, you will make a very good living indeed. The group of four romance authors I know? They're making $10k a month. Each. Their canon is strict. Their stories are consistent. And their writing is sound.

Another option under roundtable is the shared universe. Take for example, Michael Anderle's Kurtherian Gambit Universe or Martha Carr's Oriceran. Authors join the group and write their own stories, adhering to canon, but the process of covers and publication goes through a central figure. This is close to a legacy publishing contract, without the overbearing weight of the traditional publisher. The books are brought to market far more quickly because they don't have to compete for paperback shelf space in a Barnes & Noble. They get covers and editing at lightning speed, and they get proofread by a large team of voracious readers. The process doesn't have to take time. Payments happen within days of when the distributor pays the publisher. I like the self-published roundtable model for a shared universe.

I don't need to go more in-depth because everything else I talk about in this volume applies to collaborating in a shared universe under the roundtable model. As an author, how do you get invited to join a shared universe? Show that you write good books, full-length novels comparable to others in the genre of the shared universe. The management of a shared universe takes a great deal of effort, so dealing with a high-risk collaborator is an unpalatable option.

Senior/Junior

If you can find an established author to work with, or if you are established and have achieved a modicum of success, this model could work wonders for your abilities and your exposure. Look at all the co-authors James Patterson has had, or Tom Clancy, Clive Cussler, and so on. The list is long and distinguished.

No matter where you are on your journey, there is always someone who is newer and less experienced. You can help them, focusing on your strengths. Dialogue? Scene setting? World-building? There are so many elements at which one can be great. I joined Michael Anderle after he'd been publishing for a year and I'd been publishing for just under, but he was wildly successful. He had discovered the secret sauce, and he shared it with me. Okay, I'll come clean. He shared it with everyone, but I benefitted from first-hand conversations regarding writing characters and emotions people could relate to.

Our Terry Henry Walton series came about because of a business reason. Michael had a period of time in his stories he needed to address because his fans wanted it. It was an instant market with a hungry readership. It was post-apocalyptic, which he did not write. He wrote the part where his characters watch the Earth get lambasted by aliens, but they chased them into space. We decided a senior/junior relationship was in order because Michael had both skills and readers. I brought the writing game (the plot and setting).

About thirty books later, we have a more evolved arrangement, an equal partnership. You know what else we have? A contract for each series. We both protect our families and the intellectual property we created. Even in the senior/junior era, I own 50% of the earnings from those titles (minus shared ad costs). Simple as that. I learned, and it has been hugely beneficial for my overall career. Michael earned from the eleven-book series, which sold extremely well.

We both won. That was an optimal example of a senior/junior relationship.

One of the most important factors in this kind of relationship is that the junior member needs to be willing to listen. You may like the sound of your voice but know that the senior player has the trump card. Understand exactly why they recommend that something be done a certain way. Maybe offer a new alternative, but don't blow them off, and don't make them play the trump card. They're probably the one pressing the Publish button. They could change it without your approval.

If you're the junior member, watch and learn. And do learn. If you're the senior member, make sure you're teaching. Don't take the manuscript, rework it, and then never give feedback. Help the junior partner understand why.

They'll become a better writer, and so will you. Remember: See, Do, Teach. Complete the learning cycle.

. . .

Mentor/Mentee

This may sound like senior/junior, and it has a lot of the same elements, but the mentee may be the one pressing the Publish button. The mentor provides guidance through questions and raising awareness. He/she doesn't serve in a dominant role. The mentee is free to do whatever with the advice given.

I've been the recipient of sage advice by an author-mentor. He didn't have time to read my whole book, but I'd send him short passages, no more than a page. He would share his impression, guessing where the story might go. It was a valuable insight into the shape of the narrative. He helped me see how to show a scene. He also pointed me in the direction of potential readers.

He didn't spend any time with which categories I selected or anything related to publishing the finished product, but I felt like he was by my side the whole time. The mentor. He asked for nothing in return except to remember him kindly when I hit the big time. Those were the kindest and most motivating words because they came from an author I respected.

The remuneration from a mentor/mentee arrangement might be payment up front or a royalty share, but most often there is no payment, as in my situation. There is only the gratification each receives from the other. In this relationship, the mentee carries the burden of making the final decisions. The mentee is in the driver's seat.

Facebook offers a program where mentors can sign up. This is not what I think of when I think of mentors. In my opinion, it is a personal relationship where the two people believe they can work together. The mentor believes in the potential of the mentee, and the mentee respects the mentor. The relationship might change over time, but it starts with a mentee needing the guidance of a mentor who has been through the war and survived.

Having a successful mentee carries a certain level of personal gratification, too. Very few authors will get a mentor. It isn't anything that can be forced since a large number of elements have to line up for the personal relationship to take shape and grow.

"Yes, Grasshopper..." I guess I'm showing my age by referencing the *Kung Fu* tv series from 1972, but it doesn't change the lessons from it. We all learn in different ways, and one of the most profound is when a mentor takes the time to share their wisdom in a way that's not dictatorial. ***Working toward the self-actualization of being an indie is a laudable goal. Your mentor isn't working with you for your current book. It is the canvas upon which your future starts to take shape.***

The mentee has to listen. The mentee has to make the decisions about what to do. The mentor has only to ask the questions. What makes that a good paragraph? Why should I care about your main character? Where is the conflict?

Hard questions, and the hard answers of introspection. That is why respect must exist. Any mentor can save themselves a great deal of grief by not mentoring. Is the easy way the right way? This quote from John F. Kennedy sums the answer up nicely.

"We choose to go to the moon in this decade and do the other things, not because they are easy, but because they are hard, because that goal will serve to organize and measure the best of

our energies and skills, because that challenge is one that we are willing to accept, one we are unwilling to postpone, and one which we intend to win."

Take a learning journey and see how far you can go.

Work for Hire and Ghostwriting

When the one who is going to do the writing is willing to get paid by the word, you have a work-for-hire arrangement. If you give them author credit, they are work for hire. If you hide who wrote the book, it's ghostwriting. Here's a super-secret—most celebrity memoirs are written by ghostwriters.

What is it worth? That is a question for the person doing the writing. A nickel a word (as of when this was written) is a common payment. Sometimes less, sometimes more, based on other factors like experience and quality.

Some bigger names charge by the manuscript. One NY Times bestseller offered a work for hire manuscript of 70k words for $30,000. The person paying the fee has to determine if they are going to earn out (recover their costs through sales). The collaborator becomes a publisher in these cases, and the work-for-hire cost is much like an advance in royalties since the writer gets paid before the book gets published. The person who contracts with a work-for-hire author assumes all the financial risk.

I personally don't use ghostwriters. I give my co-authors credit. I've attached a sample contract (Appendix B-4) that I use. I pay a bonus of 10% over a certain earnings figure per book because I believe having long-term skin in the game is important.

The publisher needs to ensure that the quality of the books meets his/her needs and those of the targeted audience. I use the term "publisher" here because that's exactly what the co-author who did the hiring has paid to become. It sounds like a legacy-publishing acquisitions editor.

The relationship with a work-for-hire author can be rather impersonal, but it is better the more personal you can make it. Treat others as you wish to be treated.

Sometimes the publisher will need to provide a full and detailed outline, and sometimes a general outline is sufficient. In rare cases, all you need to do is talk through a story or series concept. These are things you need to work out ahead of time or as the writer starts working. During the process, reviews are important to keep the writer on track. You don't want to get a full manuscript that isn't what you expected. Rewriting a badly written story is not what you paid for. I am doing that right now on a project for a deceased author's family. I did not pay close enough attention as the story was being written, so now I get to invest a great deal more time rewriting it. I paid in both money and time. That's less than optimal.

See the theme I keep pushing? Shared expectations. Make sure your work-for-hire author is delivering what you want, and you need to be open. The other author is not you. They can try to write like you, but they won't get it exactly right. The good news is that you can double-check it and punch it up (clean up the text, rewrite, add words). Then it will be the you that your readers expect.

And that is why you hire another writer through work for

hire. You get the book without having to do all the work. I know Nora Roberts writes all her words. That is her business model. Mine pulls in co-authors in all different types of relationships to give them a chance to show their stuff, and hopefully, kickstart their careers.

Anthologies and Box Sets

These are more business collaborations than authoring collaborations. Everyone writes their own stuff and no one else gets the credit, but they are put together in one marketing package. I've included a sample contract B-5 for these so you can see how the individual authors retain their rights.

I've been involved with a number of these, a dozen anthologies and maybe five collaborative box sets. An anthology will have a theme, and authors with stories that meet that theme will submit. The best stories will be included. All the authors share the promotion on social media or to their lists. The organizer might run some ads. This is a low to no-cost way to make some money and add to your backlist. Many people write a story that could be used as a reader magnet and give it away for free. I personally write standalone short stories. I'm trying to perfect my craft, and I can do that better with shorts.

Important safety tip: make sure all the submissions are original and have never been published or risk the wrath of Amazon.

New writers who get a shot at an anthology get added exposure. In the anthologies I organize, I always ask a few established authors to join in, and have had good luck getting big names on board. Newer authors get exposed to the established author's readers. If the story sells them, congratulations! That's why I also make it a requirement that people have books in that genre, too. Readers who like their work need to have something else they can buy. Anthologies don't work if you're trying to test the waters. You'll never know if they loved your story or not. You won't pick up new readers because they are a fickle bunch who want their reading fix *now*. If you can't provide that, they'll forget you exist.

To make the most of an anthology, you need to write a great story that sells the reader in the first paragraph. You want them to read the story from start to finish without taking a break. That is how you gain new fans, and how you keep old ones.

Box sets are bundles of finished books. You don't need any others, but you have to have a book cover that is of comparable quality to the books in the box set. I am putting some of these together, and just like the anthologies, I want a mix of old and new to maximize everyone's gain.

Anthologies and box sets are collaborative efforts, but not collaborations in the sense of creating new content. These are taking original content and repackaging it for a two-pronged business purpose—make money and increase readership.

The bottom line

Every collaboration is a business arrangement. At the end of the day, it's your business and your brand. Risk. Reward. Cash flow. Those need to be taken into consideration before signing on the bottom line. It is a serious and committed business arrangement. Treat it as such, and give the relationship the respect it is due.

Keeping everything aboveboard is the best business advice I can give. Collaborations can be part of personal and business growth. Know when to wear your artist hat and when to put on your business suit. In the end, you might find that the whole is greater than the sum of its parts.

4

ESTABLISHING EXPECTATIONS OF WORK AND DELIVERY

- **Workload**
- **Deliverables**
- **Schedule and meeting deadlines**
- **Money (and Time) Investment**

This section might be a rehash of what's above, but I do that to reinforce these important details. They speak to shared expectations, and that's what I provide in Appendix B-1. It is food for thought as you break out who is responsible for what.

Self-published authors understand the burden of having to do it all yourself. Or maybe it's the freedom to control all that is within your control. I see it as freedom, but it's still nice to get help. Knowing exactly what that help looks like can relieve a burden. It's easier to carry a heavy weight when you have two people.

Let's look at what you need to allocate.

. . .

Workload

It starts with the story concept. That is some of the most fun people have with the story. It's the brainstorming and idea generation for a great tale. Capture that, and then what?

Are you building a new world? Then you have to develop some details. Whether you do that within your writing program (Scrivener, for example, has a way to track world elements), in a spreadsheet, in a personal wiki, or some other way, make sure you allocate who does what. You can both do it. Google Sheets/Docs make real-time collaboration and information updates seamless. It's an easy way to create a ready reference you both can use to ensure consistency.

Are you going to use an outline? Who writes it? That's another opportunity for clarity.

The manuscript. This is the product you will eventually put up for sale. How are you sharing the writing duties? I've done collaborations where I wrote everything and submitted it for review and discussion. I've done others where I was the reviewer. And I've done a couple where we wrote every other chapter.

The writing is a big share of the workload until it's done, and then it will disappear into the past. This is why it's important to separate the post-product workload before the book is written. Again, to keep the collaborators on the same page.

Editing, cover, blurb, keywords, and ad copy. Running ads (both who runs them and the cost), promotions. Here's a cool table to give you an idea of how it might look where P is the publication date.

	% Author 1	% Author 2	$ Author 1	$ Author 2	When
Concept	50	50			P-90
Outline	100	0			P-89
Manuscript	90	10			P-45
Book Title	50	50			P-45
Rewrite	10	90			P-30
Cover	0	100		$500	P-30
Ad Graphics	0	100			P-30
Edit	0	100		$750	P-15
Rewrite	0	100			P-10
Ad Copy	50	50			P-10
Blurb	50	50			P-10
Keywords	10	90			P-10
Formatting	0	100			P-10
Send ARCs	50	50		$50	P-10
Publish	0	100			P
Amazon Ads	0	100		$1000	P
Facebook Ads	50	50	$500	$500	P
BookBub Ads	0	100		$250	P+7
Other Ads	50	50			P+7
Typos/ Updates	50	50			P+?
Royalties	0	100			P+2 months
Promotions	0	100		$250	P+90

But you still need to work out the details of what fifty percent means, or ninety. One hundred is clear, with the delivery date. Maybe the breakout is one person does the ad work, but the other pays. It's all good. Use anything that makes sense in your particular partnership. Capture it and memorialize it in writing, so you can ultimately deliver a great product to your readers without creating internal friction.

Shared expectations with a solid business plan. That is how the whole is greater than the sum of the parts. By the third book, you are both rolling, just in time to dissolve your partnership and go your separate ways. And that's good too, as long as you know the numbers and where the continued payments are coming from. No surprises.

In a friendly engagement where you're having fun, you still need to know who is doing what to make sure you don't duplicate effort. Remember the Traveling Wilburys? They were a band made up of all-stars who got together to make a couple of albums. Were they having fun? You can tell that with Album 1 and Album 3. There was no Album 2. And we bought both of the albums because they were great. Having fun can make you a lot of money.

Deliverables

I'm a big fan of SMART goals. Every deliverable needs to be defined with a goal that is:

- Specific—Be exact. Write the outline for Book One
- Measurable—Words or chapters are easily counted. Twenty chapters of 2500 words each, an outline of 2500 words total
- Attainable—Is writing an outline viable? Probably
- Relevant—Is this the outline you need for the next phase of your project?
- Timely—Finish in one day, two, or what?

Here's what it looks like:

"I'll email you a first draft twenty-chapter outline for our Book One by tomorrow morning."

It's not difficult, but we have to know what is expected.

"I'll do it!" That statement creates an ambiguity—you'll do

what by when? Shared expectations. Make sure you embrace them to reduce any opportunity for creating friction.

In the self-publishing business, what are the deliverables? It's far more than just the manuscript. See the table above that shows a workload breakout. You'll have internal deliverables and external deliverables.

Internals are everything you need to accomplish. It might be something as simple as "tighten the language of the action in Chapter 18 by tonight."

Externals are those physical factors readers will see.

It all starts with a cover to get the readers to take the next step. The blurb. I've read some recent studies that suggest the blurb is what sells the book. There are one-click (buy with one simple click) covers, to be sure, but the blurb will sway those who look deeper. The manuscript. The ad copy. Ad graphics and ad keywords (targeting). Those are all things that need to be done and ready for use. Arguably, the ad keywords and targeting can be done last-minute, but there's generally a better return if you've been more deliberate about it, researching the categories with the best chance of finding readers who will like your book.

The best thing to do? Make a list. Insert due dates, and build in a little extra time, just in case. And check those boxes as you finish things. Once again, Google sheets or Slack or a different online tracking program will help keep both of you on the same page. Everything will be ready when it needs to be ready, or when you know you'll have it.

I've only had a cover hold up a book one time, and that was early in my career. Now I strive to have the cover done before I start writing. I write the blurb as I'm writing the book. It's not a synopsis, but a catchy one-liner, some grabby text, and a call to action. Simple as that. I keep mine short, which means no wasted words. Set the hook and reel them in. Don't play with the reader by dragging out your blurb. Don't give them a chance to not buy your book. They have to know more! One click...

Deliverables. Get the little ones done ahead of time and stay on track for the big ones. Cover and manuscript are the biggest, followed by making sure you have the editing part lined up. Control what's in your control, like time. Don't create a time crunch for your cover artist or editor (if you use them). Give them a head's up when you will need their services.

And because I want to make sure you don't miss any of the biggies, here's a list of the very basic deliverables. Everything else falls under these major groups. Are you running a huge release party? That's ads and reserving space and is all within your control.

In your control:

- Blurb
- Manuscript
- Ad copy and launch day marketing
- Graphics (maybe or not, depends on your graphic skills)
- Ad targeting (includes category and genre selection for your book)
- Formatting (unless you contract this out)

Within your ability to influence (but not control):

- Cover (and graphics if you don't do them yourself)

- Editor (if you hire an editor)

How many copies are you going to give away as advanced reader copies (ARC)? Twenty? Three hundred? Agree with your collaborator before you give them to all your readers and there's no one left to buy your book. I don't do ARCs at all, so this point is usually not up for discussion, except with my anthologies (that sample contract is Appendix B-5). I'll let the contributing authors send out up to ten copies of their individual stories before publication. Once the anthology is published, no more giveaways, and I ask the author if their reviewers are willing to buy the book so the review will show as a registered purchase. ARCs are a different conversation for a different day. They could be a source of friction between collaborators, so it's best to get that out of the way before you write the book.

Just like delivering ARCs and asking those readers to leave reviews, professionals deliver on time. It's easier to manage your business that way. Don't let "artist you" dominate "business you" (or vice versa). Deliver your deliverables.

Schedule

This section is going to be short. Make a schedule that works for you and add fifty percent to the duration because things happen in life. Better to deliver early than late. If you know you can write a book in four weeks, promise it in six. Under-promise and over-deliver.

Plan backward based on where your production bottlenecks may be. For example, the cover designer you use is backed up for six months. Guess what? You either wait six months or more for a cover or you find a different cover designer. Or you do both, planning to re-cover the book once you get the great artist's version. That's a business decision. Don't cavitate over it. Do you want to sell your book now or in six months? Business hat. Wear it and make wise decisions. Is the alternate cover good enough? Make sure the blurb is great, then go forth and make money.

Editors can sometimes hold up books unless you reserve their time early. The good editors are in high demand or will be once people find out how good they are. And then you may have to wait. Build that into your delivery and release schedule.

Schedule your promotions. Many promo sites have a two-month lead time. If you're running a sale and want to hit a paid list like Book Barbarian (for science fiction & fantasy), you'll need to lock in your slot well in advance. You can do it without an ASIN if you have a track record of success and have advertised with them before. If you haven't, you can do a long pre-order on Amazon and get your ASIN that way. Make sure you have Amazon's lockdown date for the preorder etched in your plan. And for planning purposes, if you have unknowns, set the pre-order date for a month longer than you need. You can always launch a pre-order early, but late gets you blocked from pre-orders for a year.

You can use the list above or dig a more detailed one out of my book on *Release Strategies*. You can do a soft launch, or you can plan heavily and do a hard launch to maximize your sales out of the gate. Either way, plan your days not for perfection, but if something goes wrong. Your fans will never be unhappy if you publish a book early.

Get your calendar and start writing because there are at least two of you doing things to get this book ready. That makes it both easier and harder. Until you've worked together and can understand what is getting done, there will be starts and stops. It won't flow smoothly. Extra time in your schedule will allow you to work through the issues without causing strife. Being up against a hard deadline like a pre-order final upload time will drive your anxiety through the roof. Don't do that to yourself.

What do you do when one collaborator bails or becomes unstable?

This is where the marriage analogy resonates the strongest. People who were once in love enough to get married become spitting angry at each other, hurling invective and spewing hatred.

Don't let it get to that point. This is a business arrangement. Make your peace and move on because getting your pound of flesh won't make you feel any better.

In a collaborative contract, you don't want to go to court if you don't have to. It will be expensive, and no one will go away happy. The remedy clause in a contract should make you comfortable that you have rights should you need to defend them, no matter the cost.

So what do you do when your collaborator ghosts you? That is, disappears in the night when he/she still owes you books? The contract is still in force. Are you going to sue the collaborator? You could. You have the contract, but suing someone is an expensive proposition. Do you want to spend $30,000 to try to recover...what? The potential of a good story? If you have to sue someone, you definitely don't want them writing your books. I would personally use the funds due to hire their replacement writer. Although that could be considered a violation of the contract, I've seen courts favor the party who did not walk away when monies owed were used to fix the problem created by the one who disappeared.

A collaborator who ghosts you is a big problem. You probably don't live in the same state, and possibly not even the same country. There might be no way to sue them. Maintain a good relationship, and if you have to walk away, then walk away and start fresh. Keep your reputation and your brand intact. As someone who tries to keep promises, it is beyond me how people could walk away without any further communication, leaving work unfulfilled. But it happens. Be ready to move on. Sometimes you have to step up and fill the void.

I'm in that situation right now. I have to write a book because a collaborator has disappeared. I fear he might have died. I won't speak ill as sometimes things happen. So instead of thinking that you were ghosted, think that the other person is in a coma. The problem isn't that they disappeared, the problem is how do you fix it? Find another collaborator. Write it or market it yourself. Extend your timeline since the book won't be done when promised. These things can all be managed. This is the self-published author business. As long as you keep working at it, nothing is the kiss of death. Keep your fans informed. Keep your distributor informed and keep charging forward.

Lamenting what you see in the rearview mirror is a waste of time. The view out the windshield is bigger and better. What you focus on is what you will create. The faster you let go of what's not working, the faster you will create something you want.

If you have disagreements that cannot be resolved, you could ask a third party to mediate your dispute. This would be informal but might help you both see a better way. Sometimes when your head is in a bad place, you can't see a way out. An extra set of eyes could be extremely helpful. Do your best to resolve your differences and wrap up your collaboration peacefully. Being angry and holding grudges is no way to live your life. It's like setting yourself on fire and hoping the smoke bothers the other guy. Put it behind you and move on.

It's also important to keep your disagreements private. Airing your issues in public doesn't look good. Even if you are completely in the right, you'll look wrong. Keep those things private. When you have a cooler head, your brand will thank you for your restraint.

Ending a collaboration

All collaborations end. Well, almost all. Moving on is natural. It's human nature. How do you do it without burning any bridges?

If you're ending your relationship before the contract is fulfilled, you'll need to amend your contract to save you both from later claims by one estate against the other. Remember that copyright is generally the life of the author PLUS seventy years. Your estate is going to be interested in making money from your intellectual property well past the time you laid down for a permanent dirt nap. That means your estate will handle your books and any collaborative works.

That's why even if you are the best of friends, you need a contract. Not for you, but for your heirs. Hopefully they aren't greedy, but money does weird things to people. Sign a great contract and keep everyone honest. You don't want your kids fighting over your money and fighting with your collaborator's kids. Your inattention to a good contract could start the Spanish Inquisition, and no one wants that.

No one.

I jest, but if you think about your contracts that way, you'll do much better with your collaborative business arrangements.

That's what happens when your contract is ongoing. In the samples I include at the end of the book, I include a renegotiation clause after three or seven years. It's an opportunity for one collaborator to buy out another when shared royalties are involved. If that happens, a bill of sale is required to surrender further claims against the book and money earned from it. If a deal can't be renegotiated, the original terms remain in effect. The worst you get is what you had, and that's what your heirs will deal with.

Before that, when the last book is written and the series complete, what do you do? You part ways, except for the money. One party will continue to pay the other (depending on the financial arrangement). Stay in touch. Share sales data. Run promotions once or twice a year. There is no reason for one to disappear on the other. You worked hard together. Give that its just desserts.

Whether the books panned out or not doesn't matter. The work was done.

If one collaborator goes their merry way without so much as a by your leave, don't worry about. I would still share data if I'm the publisher. If the publisher does not, watch the book ranks and try to stay engaged. After the initial run and earn-out (making back your investment), it's all gravy. Sometimes with your backlist, it's a lot of gravy.

As long as it's continuing to make money, there's no reason to be strangers. Still, there's not much you can do if you were only business partners and never friends. That will be obvious at the end. And it's okay. You're not going to get along with everyone. It's best to keep moving on, with reminders to check when royalties that you are getting paid are due if you have that type of collaborative arrangement.

If you've done ghostwriting or work-for-hire, your separation at the end of the collaboration will be much cleaner. After the publisher has paid for the words, that's it. The writer hopes they've done a good enough job to get a testimonial or more work, or maybe a different collaborative arrangement with shared royalties.

That's why it's important to never burn a bridge. If you've written something as a collaborator and go your own way, wouldn't it be nice to get a newsletter share or something from your old business partner? It can't hurt if they are willing to help an old friend.

For those people like me who collaborate a lot, make sure you keep track of when contracts come due for renegotiation. You don't want to miss something important.

And you don't want to forget to pay people if you owe them. I usually pay royalties one month ahead, as soon as I definitively know what they are. It gives me a cushion in case I do miss a month. That way I'm never late. I could pay people quarterly, although I also don't think it's right to hold onto other people's earnings. But I am the anomaly in this. Most often, you'll get a quarterly payout or a one-time payout and then earn it back (like a legacy publishing advance).

There is one strategy for ending a collaboration, and that is to go away with a smile and a handshake. Anything less will lead to friction you don't need, unhealthy levels of stress, and an aversion to trusting people. None of us want that. Shake hands. It's better that way.

Time to move on to the fun stuff.

Money and business.

5

THE BUSINESS SIDE

- **Publishing**
- **Handling the money**
- **One person**
- **Shared**
- **Separate business account**
- **Tax implications**

Publishing

These are some of the easiest things to agree to and the hardest things to swallow. "I'll write the book and you sell it" sounds good...until the book doesn't sell. You might think the other person is not pulling their weight. They didn't invest the time to write the book, so they aren't committed. Angst! Fury!

But when publishing, in the immortal words of the Highlander, there can only be one. Only one person or entity gets to hit the Publish button. Only one person or entity receives the revenue from the book. Amazon does not break it out farther than that. You need to decide who gets to press Publish. As long as all the authors are listed, you'll get your author credit and associate rank earned from sales.

An alternative to the one-publisher model is to create a publisher, your own business, formed according to your state (or country) laws, with its own tax liability. You create a new entity, and that entity sets up its own publishing account with Amazon or any of the other distributors. That entity can own the copyright, or the individuals can retain it. This isn't a sell-your-soul-to-the-devil arrangement.

Can a separate corporation for each collaborator be worth it? There is some expense and management time involved in setting up any corporate entity. It might be worth it if your titles make a great deal of money, but how do you know that ahead of time?

You don't. The separate entity is a way to protect the owners (collaborators) from each other as well as the greater world, even though individual copyright holders have the same rights as corporations. Probably more when it comes to protecting your work. I personally wouldn't go to this extreme. If your contract is sound, you're protected in a collaborative arrangement if you must go to court to defend your rights. If an individual member sues a corporation, you're spending your own money on both sides of the case.

Back to one person hitting Publish. It doesn't matter who does it. The person who presses the button will then be responsible for sharing the sales number, but the person responsible will be the only one with access to Amazon advertising (as of this writing, the ad accounts showed all the books for a publisher should a collaborator be added to the advertising account, not just the books that the collaborator is named on). And that means the advertiser is the one who foots the bill for the ads. Publishing is the money side. The publisher receives the data and the money, but the publisher is also the one who spends the money. This is more than just an Amazon issue. It is similar with all distributors. Anyone can advertise books on Facebook or BookBub. You don't need to be the publisher. That's only the case on Amazon, but savvy advertisers leverage Amazon, as well as the other ad platforms.

No one will buy your book if they don't know it's there. It doesn't matter who hits the publish button, but they are taking the financial responsibility for the collaboration.

Handling the money-expenses

Money is the thing most married couples argue about. Remember when I said a collaboration is like a marriage? It is. What if you spent two months of your life writing a spectacular trilogy, but your collaborator, the one responsible for marketing it, is only spending $5 a day? Is that what your time was worth?

Back to the contract, and then onward to a little transparency. I had a collaboration that did okay. We had decent continued sales, but it wasn't a breakout. In order to maintain the sales, I was spending 100% of my 50/50 cut because I felt bad that we weren't gaining runaway traction. And that's good. I shared the numbers multiple times a week. Since I was the one who published the book, only I saw the raw numbers of the sales and my ad spend. It was important to me to be open about everything. The books were and are great. They'll provide revenue for a long time to come.

Shared expectations. What kind of ad spend is two months of your life worth? If you share costs, make sure you agree on the spend rate and any increases before they happen. What about return on investment (ROI)? That goes to cash flow. What is acceptable to spend today for a payout in two months? Being open about the money and being transparent about what you're doing are two things that will keep collaborators from going to war. No secrets, especially about paying or getting paid. It's the secret to happiness.

The cover costs. Editing costs. Sometimes proofreaders cost. Sometimes we pay for formatting. All of these potential costs or savings need to be documented. One collaborator has Vellum. Great! Take responsibility for the book's formatting. Sign up and deliver the cost savings.

It's a bit like horse-trading, but since you will have already talked, that stuff is on the table. Have fun with it. Of course, you can do it all virtually. Let's break down the three ways to handle the money.

- One individual covers the expenses
- Sharing/parsing expenses
- An entity is formed with seed money to cover expenses

One individual

One of the collaborators paying the bills is comparable to the legacy publishing model, even if that collaborator is doing their share of the writing, too. They can then split the costs with their collaborator or take the costs out of revenue. Recovering the costs later can go to cash flow, and might hold up some of your advertising if one of you doesn't have a war chest of cash.

"I just paid $500 for the cover, can you send me $250?" Nothing like good communication. The collaborator sends the $250, notes it in their expenses for tax purposes, and gets back to doing what they're doing.

What if you only agreed on a cover that would cost $200? Now you have a problem. That's where your contract comes in. You'll see that the cover cost is detailed as part of a number of the sample contracts in the appendices. Being hit with a different cost than you expect and approved ahead of time is not good. Shared expectations and transparency are important to any healthy relationship. Don't commit the extra funds without getting your collaborator's agreement unless you're willing to cover the extra costs to keep the relationship happy and healthy.

In my case, money wasn't an issue. We talked, committed, and paid the bills directly. When I received an invoice, I paid it immediately. I didn't let anything linger. It's not good for business to risk being late with a bill. And sometimes, paying the $50 here or there is easier than trying to share those expenses. If it's because $50 is hard-earned and not readily available, make sure you have everything estimated and addressed ahead of time.

Shared expectations. Covers, editing, and all other costs. Estimated, and both sides ready to make it happen. In the legacy publishing world, the big-name publisher takes a massive chunk of the royalties to cover their costs. It is what you pay them because they're taking the risk and they are out the money up front. Same with a collaborator who hires authors under a ghostwriter or work-for-hire relationship. Same with a collaborator who covers all the costs to be recouped from royalties.

The principle is the same. One person invests and hopes for a return on that investment. As a collaborator who is not investing the money but committing their time, you have value, and an obligation to do the best job you can do. I use phrases like "churn out the words" and "hammer the keyboard." Those are self-deprecating. I hope every author tells their story in the best way possible, making each new sentence better than the last as they constantly improve their prose. I've co-written a book with Larry Martin that you'll find in the *Successful Indie Author* series (*Collaborations* is Book 3 and *Write Compelling Fiction* is Book 4). Book 4 might be worthwhile if your readers aren't fanatical about your words.

Pay your bills. If your collaborator can't, then you must, because your reputation is now on the line. ***Collaborations paint both authors with the same brush. Make sure it's a color you like.***

Shared

Sharing costs is another methodology, subtly different from the one-collaborator-pays-all model. "The bill is $500 for the cover. Send me your $250 and I'll pay the designer." This allows for collaborators who don't have a war chest of publisher cash to pay the bills. The cost-sharing happens before the bill is paid. There is no combined PayPal account or kitty into which you've thrown money. You both maintain your own funds, and pool your money only when the bill is due, and only for each bill as it comes in. You try to keep your costs to a minimum so you don't nitpick each other's wallet.

What if one of you can design a compelling cover? That could be negotiated in cost savings or writing time or royalty split. You do the cover, we'll split the editing cost 50/50, and then for royalties, you get 55% to my 45%. Don't underestimate your value. Don't overestimate it, either. Is a cover worth 10% of all royalties into the future? If the book earns nothing, no one cares since ten percent of zero is zero. The problem comes when the book is a runaway bestseller and makes a million dollars. Now that cover earned a hundred thousand. That's a spendy cover. Keep these things in mind when negotiating, and always be aboveboard.

Personal honor goes out the window when big numbers are thrown at people. Don't be that person. Don't let greed create someone you can't look at in the mirror. Up front and in the contract is where you decide these things and sign up for them. Like a marriage, it's for better or worse. Don't let "better" destroy you.

The optimal methodology in regard to low cost and responsiveness is to each take certain bills. In a couple of my collaborations, I've taken the cover cost and my collaborator handles the editor, or vice versa. In some, I've covered both and handled a share of the writing in order to get a higher cut of the royalties, upward of 75/25. But all that was negotiated up front. Shared expectations.

Separate business account

Besides simply taking on tasks and the financial

responsibility, you can also establish a budget and contribute to the pot. Take care that you trust your collaborator with your money. You can pay bills from your pile as they come in, or you can establish a joint account under a unique LLC (driving your overhead costs up) and pull money from there. But once again, you'll need to trust your collaborator implicitly. What if they spend without seeding the pot? Freak out!

No, don't freak out, but all revenue and expenses need to be accounted for. The hardest conversations are the ones that start with, "I think there's some money missing..."

That will lead to a marriage (collaboration) that won't end well. Trust but verify. Keep the important things on the table until the collaborators have earned each other's trust.

I mentioned an LLC above. Setting up a company takes a few steps and has a number of costs. I recommend Joe Solari's book *The Business Owner's Compendium* to help you on the business side of the business. One of the reasons to collaborate is to partner with someone who has their business ducks in a row. That saves time and effort. Forming a business umbrella under which to collaborate is a complex effort and requires its own book. I would say it's more viable if you go long term, almost like a real marriage.

You'd better like your collaborator a lot to commit to that level of business partnership.

Handling the money—revenue

What is your time worth? If I take eighty hours to write a book, what commitment is required from my collaborator to review and then sell that book? If this is a work-for-hire arrangement, you've negotiated that value right up front. A nickel a word, maybe more, maybe less. If you are splitting revenue, you'll need to work out those numbers.

If I can sell a thousand copies at full price the first week the book is out, is that worth your time to write the book? Residual sales, and a long sales tail. In other words, how quickly will the book earn out? That is the value of time. The longer it takes to recoup costs, the lower the value. We want a big number! Is $250/hour too much, or a good target? It's the one I use to gauge my writing time's value. This is what I need a book to earn in the first ninety days to be worthwhile.

Lower than that has resulted in ending a series early, wrapping at four books instead of eight. Remember, this is a business. You can love writing the characters, but you and your collaborator need to put food on the table. $250 isn't an arbitrary number for me. It's what I made in my days as a lawyer-turned-business-consultant. It's my constant target, but now I'm not on the road more than 50% of my life. I prefer now. Collaborations helped make it all possible.

Back to revenue. Whoever presses Publish is the one who gets the revenue (unless your LLC publishes, and then you can both have access to the account because your collaborations will be the only books in there). Then you split it.

But! There are companies out there like BundleRabbit or Draft2Digital's Shared Worlds program. You can publish books through them and they'll split the revenue however you determine. They do this for a certain cut of the revenue, something like 10-15%. There will be a time lag between when the money is sent to them and when they turn it around to you. You'll need to accept that if you sign up with their services, but you'll be comforted by knowing you'll get your designated cut, calculated to the penny.

PublishDrive's Abacus Tool will calculate your shared earnings based on your royalty reports, making the data available to each of your collaborators. They'll normalize the values based on exchange rates and give you the exact amounts owed each. With PublishDrive, you are paying for their data parsing. The publisher is still the one who will receive the revenue and then have to make the payments.

This side of the business is best handled as friends working together, sharing the financial burden and reaping the monetary reward. There will be two times when money is a problem: when you don't have any, and when you have too much. These are the financial crises that try people's souls.

Have we talked about money and time enough? Shared expectations. Everything up front. Make a list. Share. Stay above board, be transparent. And keep your eyes on the prize—selling a great book.

Taxes

Which leads to taxes. If you are in the United States and you're paying a collaborator their share of royalties, it's best to have a W-9 on record and send them a 1099-MISC at the end of the year with the totals. It makes it easier to write off and easier for them to account for. If your collaborators are multi-national, your PayPal or transfer receipt is usually enough to hold the IRS at bay. UK and Canadian authors will pay their taxes based on that income. If you're paying directly, there won't be any withholding unless the publisher (the collaborator under whose account the book was published) holds it back, and that's a lot of forms.

There are W8-BENs, W-4s, and so many more. You need to hire a tax professional to make sure you are not getting yourself into tax trouble. Nothing will destroy your creative energy more than being audited. I was, and it sucked mightily. I failed to check one box on a dissolution form, and that was what triggered it. I keep good records and passed the audit with flying colors, so it was good in the end, but those were a rough couple of weeks.

Make sure your tax stuff is square. You'll get one hundred percent of your royalties, and it will be incumbent upon you to pay The Man his cut. It sucks, but the last thing you want to do is run afoul of your tax authorities. And in Australia? Holy crap, they have some challenging tax statutes. Hire an accountant who knows about self-publishing. And the state *will* take their cut. Make no mistake about that.

Account for your own revenue, but only pay taxes on your half. Don't overpay! Uncle Sam doesn't need to get a free loan from you.

You'll both be able to deduct your expenses, as long as you made more money than you spent. This is the point that separates a business from a hobby. You only need to make one dollar more than you spend. Sure, you can take a loss as a carry-over from year to year, but you can only do that a limited number of times before you have to dissolve your business or get slammed in back taxes for deductions that are retroactively disallowed.

Business. Not a hobby. Keep it that way. Manage the business to earn a profit.

Each collaborator can deduct expenses, and this is why I prefer the model where I pay for the editing, you pay for the cover, and we'll each pay for our own ads. The money evens out in the end. Accepting payments from your collaborator means you have to account for those somehow as revenue you'll then deduct later. It gets cumbersome, but it can be done.

6

CONTRACT DETAILS

- **Contract terms to look out for**
- **Details**
- **Something fun**

Contract terms to look out for

This is going to be a short section since we don't need to belabor contracts. I don't want to bore the snot out of you. I took a number of contracts classes in law school. That was some sexy and exciting stuff, but then, I'm a complete alien. I know that stuff isn't for everyone, so let me try to boil it down to the simplest terms.

Details—know what you're contracting for. This is the Who (including legal jurisdiction under which the contract was written), What, When, How, and possibly Why.

Who. Make sure that you and your collaborator are clearly identified, your businesses, your home location (that can change without an amendment, as long as a court can track down that you are you). "I, Craig Martelle of Craig Martelle, Inc, an Alaskan Corporation..."

What. The work product you are developing must be clearly identified, as well as what it consists of. "A manuscript of at least 60,000 words, written in third person omni in the shared universe known as Craigsylvania." This can also be included as the Scope.

When. When is the product to be produced? "by October 4th, 2019." This also includes the duration of the contract, which will be a separate clause.

How. I put this in my contracts as I work in Microsoft Word. I was once handed a story that had been done in Pages and the person didn't know how to convert it. Having a story that is unreadable helps no one and shouldn't satisfy the contract deliverable.

Other tools are available for online collaborating, like Dropbox and Google Docs. If that's what you like to use, then negotiate it as part of the contract. Ensure you have shared expectations.

Why. I put this in when I'm justifying an extended duration of exclusivity or simply stating the purpose of the collaboration. In some contracts, this would be called precatory language, words that are unenforceable. We did a list-builder where a group of us put ten stories on BookFunnel in a single package for users to download, but they had to give us their email address, which was then added to each of our individual subscriber lists. The contract language said exactly that. Your book will be given away for free. There will be no money, but you shall realize nirvana when handed a list of a thousand new subscribers. I left out the nirvana part, but you get the idea. It's about having shared expectations. Here's exactly what we're doing, and why.

Shared terms

Terms used within the contract. Sometimes this is a separate section, but more often, it is clarified after the identifying criteria. "This Agreement is being made on MONTH, DAY, YEAR by and between ________________, hereinafter known as ("Publisher"), a corporation incorporated in STATE located at COMPANY ADDRESS, and FIRST LAST a.k.a. PEN NAME, hereinafter known as ("Collaborator"), an individual located at ADDRESS, CITY, STATE, COUNTRY..."

The Money

Besides the identifying criteria of who, what, and when, this is the most important part of the contract. It details who pays and who gets paid. If your book doesn't sell, no one cares about these details, but what if you pass away and your heirs get a movie deal for your story? You'd better have these contract elements correct and clear. Ambiguous statements have a tendency to get ruled on harshly by the courts and may not deliver what the collaborator intended.

Expenses as well as revenue must be covered somewhere in your contract. It's not something to beat someone up with, but for shared expectations. Transparency. All the collaborators doing what they are supposed to.

Copyright and authorship credit

This has overlapping implications with the money. Maybe a company wants to turn your sweet romance into a hardcore porno. As a copyright owner, you can keep that from happening. You have a say (unless you sign that away by giving the publisher the sole authority to determine derivative rights). If this is important to you, then don't sign away your derivative (other media and related revenue streams that aren't exactly the identified published product. This is usually movie rights from the book) rights. And make sure your name is annotated properly.

If you use a pen name, you'll need to be sure the contract has both your real name and your pen name (unless you've developed your pen name through a corporation, but at some point, your real name has to be associated with your pen name in case you ever have to go to court to protect your rights). If your pen name gets the copyright, that's fine, as long as you have a contract to show that's you. Too many people flippantly use pen names. Don't do that. Each pen name is its own unique entity. Treat it as such.

Warranties and indemnification

These clauses are to ensure that one party is protected in case the other does something untoward, like copy passages from other books and pass them off as original. That's theft of intellectual property, and it's not a good look on an author. If a collaborator does that, the indemnification clause puts the legal liability on the individual and not the collaborators together.

Remedies

This is the first thing I look for in any contract. What do I do when things go south? The bigger the corporation, the more restrictive your rights may be. The contract to use Amazon, for example, contains an arbitration clause. You can't be forced into arbitration, but the contract requires you to jump through some hoops to get out of that clause, and those things must be done *before* the incident in which you find yourself at odds.

Contracts without remedy clauses are not good. I've signed a number of contracts with cover artists where the cover artist has all the rights. I usually make pen changes (annotated additions before the contract is signed that serve as legal addenda where remedies apply equally to both parties. Contracts that are grossly one-sided because one party is in a superior bargaining position are called contracts of adhesion. Courts don't like them, and penalize the party writing the contract if the subjected party takes legal action.

So don't do that. Apply remedies equally in case either party fails to uphold their end of the contract. It's pretty crappy that these have to be in there, but it's necessary because too many have not kept their promises. That's all a contract is—a memorialized promise. It's like JK Rowling's Unbreakable Vow without the death-if-you-don't-comply part.

Moral rights

Are you willing to give up artistic license? Moral rights are your ownership of your story idea, or at least your share of the ownership as a collaboration. The example above was a clean romance turned into hardcore porn. With your moral rights intact, you can prevent that from happening. Your story remains your story. Legacy publishing often restricts an author's moral rights. The story you write might not be the one that gets published. They'll do what they think will sell the best. You will generally not have moral rights in ghostwriting or work-for-hire collaborations.

Sign and date

This finalizes the agreement. Without a signed and dated copy, there is no agreement. The date is important in case of legal action. Anything that falls after the date of the contract is subject to the contract terms, such as payments. It also starts the clock ticking on deliverables like the manuscript, or responsibility for paying for the cover or editing.

And there you go—a basic primer on contracts. The appendices are copies of contracts for your reference. These do not constitute legal advice. They can always be worded better, but there is a certain "good enough" factor. The best way to comply with any contract is to become friends with your collaborator, then give and take in a healthy way through shared expectations and transparency. The contract is for your heirs.

If you use these contracts without consulting your lawyer, you use them at your own risk. Always consult a lawyer before entering into a legal contract.

Something fun

While I was going through law school, I studied from 3AM to 8AM every morning and then played nine holes of golf. It's important for your brain to unwind after hours of reading mind-numbing legalese. A couple of fellow authors started a jibe regarding being able to do well in any genre as long as the story is well written. Here was the exchange and my response.

Captain's Log: Mark Dawson started this with Diane Capri in a question about whether anyone can do well in a certain genre. The answer is not only yes, but hell yes. Any genre can be lucrative if you hit it and act like you belong there. I am continually ranked among all the big names in science fiction and have been continuously since March 6, 2017. Michael Anderle is at the front, almost perennially at science fiction's number one position.

Any genre, if you embrace it as your own.

I bring you...*Dirty Dinos*, a collaboration with Mark Dawson.

Velocirapture

We couldn't stop. The light in the sky added heat to our passion.

Mark: Wait. Are you talking the meteor?

Craig: Some climax, huh?

Mark: Think sequel. How do we write a sequel to our mega-million bestseller?

Craig: Word. Let me start again.

We couldn't stop. The light in the sky added heat to our passion.

Mark: That's the same thing you wrote before.

Craig: But this time it's not a meteor.

Mark: Pray continue.

Craig: She gathered the boys, like the good queen she was.

Mark: Wait. Is this Velocirapture or Reverse Velocirapture?

Craig: He stood tall and proud, clicking and honking his claims to the pride, his reptilian hide glistening with the morning rain. A distant call answered his. A competitor.

Mark: Looking good. A little action. Maybe we can throw in a hunt, make it a dino-thriller.

Craig: That's so Jurassic. I'm thinking Triassic. And Velocirapture. A little action indeed! Open-door steamy since, well, no doors.

Mark: Pray continue.

Craig: He vaulted from the boulder, landing roughly, his eight-inch claws digging deep into the mossy turf. The pride bobbed their heads in appreciation of his rippling muscles and six-pack abs.

Mark: Wait. Six-pack abs?

Craig: I hear it's all the rage.

Mark: No six-pack. Think dino-kegger.

Craig: I like where you're going...

This is fiction; there is no collaboration. But there could be, if only...

. . .

Thank you for picking up this book. I hope you found it informative and helpful as you strive to reach that next level in your self-publishing career.

BIBLIOGRAPHY

As books from these good people change over time, I'm going to list just the main ones that I have. Check out their Amazon author page to see what else they have in their bag of supporting tricks.

Joe Solari
Business Owner's Compendium: A practical guide to the theory of starting, owning and operating a business
https://www.amazon.com/dp/B0728G3T7N
Joe's Author Page
https://www.amazon.com/Joe-Solari/e/B01MZ4KOPM/

Kevin J. Anderson & Rebecca Moesta
Writing as a Team Sport
https://www.amazon.com/dp/B07F8BZL5Q

Rhett C. Bruno & Steve Beaulieu

Two Authors, One Book: Co-Writing
https://www.amazon.com/dp/B07BMKLKC4

Tammi Labrecque
Newsletter Ninja: How to Become an Author Mailing List Expert
https://www.amazon.com/dp/B07C6J8HP9
Tammi's Author Page
https://www.amazon.com/Tammi-Labrecque/e/B00Q7RSPEI/

Brian Meeks
Mastering Amazon Ads, @2017
https://www.amazon.com/dp/B072SNXYMY
Mastering Amazon Descriptions, @2019 https://www.amazon.com/dp/B07NSH2QLM
Brian's Author Page on Amazon https://www.amazon.com/Brian-D.-Meeks/e/B0073XZH78/

David Gaughran
Let's Get Digital: How to Self-Publish and Why You Should, @2018
https://www.amazon.com/dp/B078ZNWD61
From Strangers to Superfans, @2018
https://www.amazon.com/dp/B0798PH9QT
BookBub Ads Expert, @2019
https://www.amazon.com/dp/B07P57V38D
David's Author Page on Amazon
https://www.amazon.com/David-Gaughran/e/B004YWUS6Q/

Mal Cooper
Help! My Facebook Ads Suck
https://www.amazon.com/dp/B078NBW3M3
Michael Cooper's Author Page
https://www.amazon.com/Michael-Cooper/e/B071FJHK9K/

Chris Fox
5000 Words Per Hour
https://www.amazon.com/dp/B00XIQKBT8
Write to Market
https://www.amazon.com/dp/B01AX23B4Q
Six Figure Author
https://www.amazon.com/dp/B01LZEM7SB
Relaunch Your Novel
https://www.amazon.com/dp/B071HVZD1G
Chris's Author Page
https://www.amazon.com/Chris-Fox/e/B00OXCKD2G/

Bryan Cohen
How to Write a Sizzling Synopsis
https://www.amazon.com/dp/B01HYBWOF6
Bryan's Author Page
https://www.amazon.com/Bryan-Cohen/e/B004I9WJTY/

Dave Chesson, Kindlepreneur
Book Marketing 101 & KDP Rocket
https://kindlepreneur.com/book-marketing-101/
Amazon Book Description Generator Tool
https://kindlepreneur.com/amazon-book-description-generator/

Mark Dawson
Learn Amazon Ads
https://www.amazon.com/dp/B06Y6BSRLR
Mark's Author Page
https://www.amazon.com/Mark-Dawson/e/B0034Q9BO8/
Mark's outstanding Self-Publishing Formula course - https://selfpublishingformula.com/

Shawn Coyne
The Story Grid: What Good Editors Know @2015
https://www.amazon.com/dp/B00WT7TP8A

Appendix A – Acronyms and Terms

ACX – Audiobooks on Amazon
AMS – Amazon Marketing Services (Amazon ads)
BB – BookBub (the gold standard paid newsletter promotion service)
ENT – eReader News Today (a paid newsletter promotion service)
KDP – Kindle Direct Publishing
KENP – Kindle Edition Normalized Page (count)
KU – Kindle Unlimited
ML – Mailing List
NL – Newsletter

Product Life Cycle – just like with any commercial product, a book has a life cycle, but it can be extended almost endlessly. The product life cycle steps are

1. Research & Development – the story idea, the plot, a series arc, the outline, and the production of the book. This also includes your preparation steps – getting beta readers, editing, book cover, blurb, categories, everything you need to publish a finished product
2. Introduction – the publication and launch process. Whether you do that through pre-orders, hard launch, or soft launch, this also includes how you've built up your reader expectations
3. Growth – advertising, marketing, adding books to the series, expanding product lines related to a book like audio, graphic novels, paperbacks, hardbacks. And more.
4. Maturity – that point when growth is stalling. The characters have seen their best days, but the opportunity to increase sales is limited.
5. Decline - Sales begin to drop and return on investment ad spend starts to decrease. Without an intentional effort to extend the product life cycle, sales will quickly decline. New covers, new blurbs, new marketing, can all extend engagement. Getting a movie deal will reinvigorate a series no matter how long it's been in decline.

APPENDIX B-1 - BREAKOUT OF ROLES AND RESPONSIBILITIES

Co-Author Writer's Agreement – breakout of roles and responsibilities (not a formal contract)

PUBLISHING AGREEMENT

This Agreement, made and entered into this ____ day of MONTH, YYYY, by and between NAME OF AUTHOR A - a.k.a. PEN NAME, hereinafter "Author A" or "Writer A" and NAME OF AUTHOR B, hereinafter "Author B" or "Writer B." This Agreement is being made on MONTH, DAY, YEAR by and between ________________ hereinafter known as ("Writer A") at address in STATE, and FIRST LAST a.k.a. PEN NAME hereinafter known as ("Writer B"), an individual located at_ADDRESS, CITY, STATE, COUNTRY__ with reference to the following facts and purposes:

RECITALS

Whereas, Author A and Author B intend to produce a mutual work product, hereinafter "Co-Authored Publication" for mutual benefit, whether in royalties or exposure; and

Whereas Author A and Author B will share expenses in the production and subsequent advertising of the Co-Authored Publication, as delineated hereunder; and

Whereas Author A and Author B will operate exclusively in this currency ____________

Whereas, Author A and Author B mutually agree to publish the Co-Authored Publication.

In consideration of the premises and mutual covenants herein contained, the parties
agree as follows:

1. CREATIVE DIRECTION

A. The creative direction of the Co-Authored Publication will be determined mutually with the final decisions made by (check one).

__ Author A

__ Author B

__ By Mutual Agreement, without which the work will not go forward and this contract is declared null and void

Author A and Author B will be listed on the Co-Authored Publication's cover and inside mutually, in order of Author A, then Author B

2. TIMING OF PRODUCTION

The work is intended to be finished by ______________ (MM/DD/YYYY) and will be produced in a mutually agreed to fashion as follows (check one).

__ Author A and Author B work on the Co-Authored Publication at the same time in a collaborative environment

__ Author A finishes Author A's section of the Co-Authored Publication in ___ days, then hands the work to Author B, who after ___ days returns Author B's completed section to Author A. The process continues until the Co-Authored Publication is completed

__ Author A and Author B produce their sections of the Co-Authored Publication independently to combine their completed sections no later than _________________ (MM/DD/YYYY).

__ Other (describe fully)

____

____

3. COST OF PRODUCTION

A. The costs of production (artwork, editing, formatting, printing, et al) will be agreed to by Author A and Author B, in writing, before such costs are incurred. Any costs incurred without mutual written consent will be paid by the incurring party, without reimbursement from the revenue of the Co-Authored Publication.

B. The costs of production will be initially paid for by and reimbursed from the initial profits received from the Co-Authored Publication.

__ Author A ___________%

__ Author B ___________ %

__ Third Party ___________ % (detail name and contact information) ________________

____

Estimated costs of production – (non-binding), include whether Author A or Author B will perform these functions (i.e. Author A creates the cover art and Author B creates the typography)

Cover Art – Cost _____________ Responsibility - __ Author A / __ Author B

Other Artwork - Cost _____________ Responsibility - __ Author A / __ Author B _

Editing (line, development, or other as mutually agreed to) -
Cost ______________
Responsibility - __ Author A / __ Author B

Formatting - Cost ______________ Responsibility - __ Author A / __ Author B

Other (describe fully) -

____

- Cost ______________ Responsibility - __ Author A / __ Author B

4. ADVERTISING AND COST OF ADVERTISING

A. Author A and Author B agree that the advertising budget for the Co-Authored Publication shall be ____________. Any changes to this amount will be agreed to, in writing before expenditures beyond this amount are incurred.

B. The costs of production (artwork, editing, formatting, printing, et al) will be agreed to by Author A and Author B, in writing, before such costs are incurred. Any costs incurred without mutual written consent will be paid by the incurring party, without reimbursement from the revenue of the Co-Authored Publication.

C. The costs of production will be initially paid for by and reimbursed from the initial profits received from the Co-Authored Publication.

__ Author A ___________%

__ Author B ___________ %

D. Advertising methods, outlets, advertisers, and other advertisements will be determined as follows.

__ Author A's sole discretion

__ Author B's sole discretion

__ Author A and B mutually agree in writing before costs are incurred

__ Author A has a budget of ______ to do with in Author A's sole discretion

__ Author B has a budget of ______ to do with in Author B's sole discretion

E. Ad copy will be produced as part of the Co-Authored Publication during production of the Co-Authored Publication.

__ Author A

__ Author B

__ By Mutual Agreement

__ Other (detail here)

----

5. DETERMINATION OF PUBLISHABILITY

A. The determination that the publication is ready to be published will be made as follows.

__ Author A

__ Author B

__ By mutual agreement, in writing between Author A and Author B

__ By a third party (detail name and contact information)

B. Once the determination is made as per 5.A. above, the Co-Authored Publication will be uploaded within ___ days by (check one)

__ Author A

__ Author B

__ By a third party (detail name and contact information)

C. The Co-Authored Publication will be published in the following distribution channels (check all that apply)

__ Amazon Kindle Select (exclusive to Amazon)

__ Amazon (wide)

__ Kobo

__ Barnes & Noble

__ iTunes

__ Smashwords

__ KDP Print

__ Other (list here)

----

6. DISPOSITION OF REVENUE

A. All data regarding sales of the Co-Authored Publication will be one hundred percent transparent to Author A and Author B as available from each distribution channel.

B. Revenue will be collected as follows.

__ Author A and Author B create a mutual business bank/credit union account into which all revenue from the Co-Authored Publication is deposited

__ Author A receives all revenue before distribution between Author A and Author B

__ Author B receives all revenue before distribution between Author A and Author B

__ A third party (detail name and contact information here) ________________________________ receives all revenue before distribution between Author A and Author B

C. Revenue will be distributed as follows.

Yes / No (circle one) Production and Advertising costs as approved according to sections 3. And 4. above will be fully reimbursed before profits are distributed.

If no, but Production and Advertising costs will be reimbursed, then describe here when and how that reimbursement take place.

____

____

D. The distribution of profits will be as follows.

__ % to Author A

__ % to Author B

E. Profit distributions will be made according to the following timeline (check one)

__ Quarterly (March 31, June 30, September 30, and December 31) for the previous quarter's distribution from publishing sites.

__ Within _____ days following profit distribution from the distribution channels

6. DERIVATIVE WORKS

A. The characters and worlds created as part of the Co-Authored Publication are the mutually inspired property of both Author A and Author B. As such, the characters are exclusive to the Co-Authored Publication. Should any derivative works be created solely by Author A or Author B, then the distributions from the revenue generated by such works shall attach as delineated in 5.D. above.

B. If Author A or Author B waives rights to derivative works, then that waiver must be detailed in a separate written agreement.

7.REMEDIES

Should a dispute arise between Author A and Author B that is not detailed above or has not been contemplated as part of this contract, the exclusive remedy is to remove the Co-Authored Publication from all distribution channels until such dispute is resolved in a written agreement by both parties.

8.CONFIDENTIALITY

Author A and Author B will maintain the contents of the Co-Authored Publication in strict confidence. Snippets and other book details will be made public through social media or other outlets as follows.

__ Author A's sole discretion

__ Author B's sole discretion

__ Author A and B mutually agree in writing

9. GOODWILL

Author A and Author B recognize the value of Goodwill associated with the Co-Authored Publication and acknowledge that all Copyrights, trademarks, and Goodwill pertaining to the Co-Authored Publication shall belong mutually to both Author A and Author B.

Author A and Author B agree to represent the Co-Authored Publication and related products in good faith and in the best interest of both parties in all public forums including social media and convention commentaries.

10. WARRANTIES OF AUTHOR

Author A and Author B hereby represents, warrants, covenants and agrees, which representations, warranties, covenants and agreements, together with all other representations, warranties, covenants and agreements of Author in this Agreement, shall be true and correct as of the date of this Agreement and shall survive the date of this Agreement, that:

A. Author is the sole and exclusive creator of any new concepts they bring to the development of the Co-Authored Publication.

B. The execution and delivery of this Agreement by Author A and Author B has been duly and validly authorized and approved by all necessary action of Author A and Author B. This Agreement is a valid and binding obligation of Author A and Author B, enforceable against either in accordance with its terms.

11. Author CREDITS.

A. Author A and Author B agrees to acknowledge, in a conspicuous place, in conspicuous type, in the published version of the Co-Authored Publication, Authors contribution to the development of the published commercial product.

B. The Co-Authored Publication will properly credit Author A and Author B as such in any work published; however, no liability shall arise by a failure or mistake to do so, although Author A and Author B agree to make a good faith effort to correct any mistake or lack of attribution in subsequent printings and by correct attribution on Author A's and Author B's website. A copyright notice for the Co-Authored Publication in the name of the Authors will be listed conspicuously within the Co-Authored Publication.

12. MISCELLANEOUS.

A. This agreement supersedes and replaces all previous agreements between the two parties concerning the Co-Authored Publication and sets forth the complete and only understanding of the Parties and cannot be changed orally.

B. This Agreement shall be binding upon and inure to the benefit of the parties hereto, and their heirs, personal representatives, successors and assigns. The rights herein shall not be assigned to a third party.

C. This Agreement may be executed in one or more counterparts, each of which when so executed shall be an original, but all of which together shall constitute one agreement.

D. If any of the provisions of this Agreement or the application thereof shall be invalid or unenforceable to any extent, it is the intention of the parties that the remainder of this Agreement and the application of such provision to other persons or circumstances shall not be affected thereby and shall be enforced to the greatest extent permitted by law. It is also the intention of the parties that in lieu of each such clause or provision of this Agreement that is illegal, invalid, or unenforceable, there be added as a part of this Agreement a clause or provision as similar in terms to such illegal, invalid or unenforceable clause or provision as may be possible and be legal, valid, and enforceable.

E. Except as otherwise provided herein, time is of the essence.

F. Author A and Author B agree to make, execute and deliver any additional documents that may be necessary to carry out this Agreement.

IN WITNESS WHEREOF, the parties hereto have executed this Agreement as of the day and year first above written.

Author A: ____________________Date: _________________

Signature: ______________________

Author B: ____________________Date: _________________

Signature: ______________________

APPENDIX B-2 - SIMPLE COLLABORATION CONTRACT

Collaboration Agreement – Short Version

For books between xx*Namexx* (**Collaborator**) and *BigName* (**Publisher**) which are collaborations written in *the list series or book or whatever here.* This contract is for *list what it's for* (trilogy, series, standalone). Here are the details:

1) We agree to split all income as follows: **Collaborator** will be paid 50% of royalties after the cost of the covers has been subtracted (covers cost $xxx each). **Publisher will receive** 50%, Income is paid by Amazon (or others if not exclusive to Amazon) for sales of books, and monthly KENP payment (should our series be in Kindle Unlimited). Payment will be made by **Publisher** to **Collaborator** within five (5) business days after Amazon (and/or other distributors used) pays **Publisher**. Publisher will provide a monthly accounting of sales and revenue to **Collaborator**. This agreement remains

in effect should one of the parties to this contract pre-decease the other. Rights will transfer to heirs or assigns as determined by competent authority. This contract is not transferable.

2) **Publisher** will pay up-front costs for the covers, formal editing, and book formatting (both digital and paperback). Only the cost of the cover shall be shared by the **Collaborator**.

3) The inside of the book is going to read something like the information below. The idea is that the Mystically Engineered universe and characters etc. etc. belong to **Publisher**, who want protection for all collaborators and understand that by listing collaborators in the front of a book they have the right to question (go to court and have rights) if someone tried to, as an example, sell the movie rights to a book and not include the collaborator in the income payment. As a note, all income for movie rights would be split as defined in paragraph 1).

TITLE (this book) is a work of fiction.
All of the characters, organizations, and events portrayed in this novel are either products of the author's imagination or are used fictitiously. Sometimes both.

This Complete Book is Copyright (c) 2019 by ***Collaborator* & *Publisher***

list series or book or whatever here (and what happens within / characters / situations / worlds) are copyright © 2019 by **Publisher and Collaborator (in shares determined in paragraph 1 above).**

4) **Publisher** shall retain sole discretion in the determination of derivative rights from this and all works using the *series name* characters and ideas. Profits from derivative works will be split as defined in paragraph 1).

5) An audiobook version may be produced (unless previous agreed otherwise) within 6 months of book release (often this is within a month - but **Publisher** does not know the future). We will split the cost of the narrator, which will also be taken out of the audio income. **Publisher** will pay the costs for the audiobook up front, and shall recover 50% of those documented costs from initial audiobook proceeds**.** Following this recovery, all further audiobook proceeds will be split as follows: **Publisher** 50% and **Collaborator** 50%.

6) No Marketing Expenses are to be apportioned by either party. While it is a smart idea to market our books, we take those expenses on separately. Both **Collaborator** and **Publisher** share in the due diligence to market the book through newsletters (both personal and swapped), social media, and paid ads.

7) This agreement is for the *xxreiterate here the title of the series and then how many booksxx.* The intent is that the manuscripts will be approximately 70,000 words in length and delivered no

more than six weeks apart starting as soon as possible. **Publisher** will provide an outline for each story to the **Collaborator**. They will be published as soon as **Publisher** determines the best window of opportunity for maximum profitability. This contract will be renegotiated should the series continue to a fourth book and beyond.

8) The term of this agreement is for seven (7) years, after which one party may buy out the others at a price to be mutually agreed upon at that time. If that does not happen within 30 days of the 7th anniversary of this agreement, the agreement will renew for an additional seven (7) years, under the same terms.

Agreed and Accepted:

Collaborator: ______________________________

Date: _______________

Publisher: _____________________________

Date: ___________________________

APPENDIX B-3 - EXTENSIVE TWO-PERSON COLLABORATION AGREEMENT

Individual and extensive collaborator agreement primarily for work for hire

INDIVIDUAL COLLABORATION AGREEMENT

This Agreement is being made on MONTH, DAY, YEAR by and between ____________________ hereinafter known as ("Publisher") a corporation incorporated in **STATE** located at **COMPANY ADDRESS**, and FIRST LAST a.k.a. PEN NAME hereinafter known as ("Collaborator"), an individual located at_ADDRESS, CITY, STATE, COUNTRY__ with reference to the following facts and purposes:

1. Publisher is a publisher of books and electronic publications. Included in Publisher's output are series of fantasy fiction based either on "universes" and/or "series" comprised of unique fictional

characters and locations contained in written materials, including, without limitation, books, but also other literary forms and materials, such as "bibles," outlines, lists of characters, chronologies, etc.) created for the purpose of developing the materials that make up the universe and/or series.

2. Collaborator is a writer of, among other genres, fantasy fiction.
3. Publisher and Collaborator agree to work together to create new characters created and owned by Publisher to serve as the basis for a series of books (the "Series"), and this Series is referenced in the schedule referenced in the attached Attachment A incorporated herein. Publisher and Collaborator desire to work together, pursuant to this agreement, for the purpose of producing written books and other materials (collectively, the "Work") which are referenced in Attachment A.

NOW, THEREFORE, in consideration of the mutual covenants contained herein, and for other good and valuable consideration, the parties agree as follows.

1. **COLLABORATION:** Publisher and Collaborator have agreed to work together for the sole purpose of producing Materials that will comprise, express and exploit the Series referenced in the attached Attachment A, incorporated herein.

1. **SCOPE:** Collaborator will write the Work based

on specifications provided by Publisher. Publisher may, in Publisher's sole discretion, use or not use the Work or any part thereof, and may make any changes in, deletions from or additions to the Work. There is no guarantee, either written or implied, regarding publication of the Work by Publisher.

1. **DURATION:** This agreement will be considered executed and legally binding from the date of the last countersignature made by either party and will be in effect for a period of seven (7) years from that countersignature date. This Agreement shall automatically renew for a subsequent two (2) years term unless either party is notified by the other in writing at least ninety (90) days prior to the end of the current term that a two year renewal is not desired. Should the agreement not be renewed and/or is terminated, both parties agree that the non-renewal or early termination shall not extinguish the obligations undertaken during the agreement term, nor the rights granted hereunder.

1. **WORK FUNDING & PROCEEDS:**

4.1 Once Publisher publishes the Work, Publisher and Collaborator will split net income after expenses, from all sources, including net income derived from other works as agreed to in writing by Publisher, to the extent same are based on the Work ("**Derivative Works**"), as follows:

1. For books written by Publisher and Collaborator, on a ratio of 00% for Publisher and 00% for Collaborator.
2. For books written by Collaborator with a source other than Publisher, on a ratio of 00% for Publisher, 00% for Collaborator and 00% for external source (such as a ghost writer). Payment of 00% to external source may be made by either Publisher or Collaborator as agreed to in writing by both parties (on a case by case basis).

4.2 The expenses that Publisher may deduct from gross receipts derived from exploitation of the Work in all media include the following:

1. Any cost for the engagement of ghost writers will be apportioned as follows;
2. If 100% costs are paid by Publisher up front, the ratio of costs reimbursement will be 50% to Publisher, 50% to Collaborator (to cover Collaborator's portion pre-paid by Publisher)
3. If 100% costs are split between Publisher and Collaborator up front, no deductions shall be made from resulting gross receipts.
4. Publisher may deduct the expenses of producing each cover of a book included in the Work up to $500 per cover (a book's cover expenses in excess of $500 shall require the written agreement of Collaborator).
5. Should Publisher decide to produce an audiobook

version, Publisher may deduct all related audio production costs including narrator, but only against receipts derived from exploitation of audiobook.

6. For physical books, Publisher may deduct the cost of the paperback layout and extensions up to $100 per paperback (these expenses in excess of $100 shall require the written agreement of Collaborator).
7. Publisher may deduct marketing costs only to the extent agreed upon in writing by Collaborator.
8. Publisher may deduct the expenses of exploiting the Work and any rights therein, and any Derivative Works, including, without limitation, commissions and fees paid to agents and lawyers.

4.3 Profits on the sale of derivative rights from books covered under this Agreement and all works using the Series characters and ideas shall be weighted as noted in the attached Attachment B incorporated herein (to account for marketing and series development costs) and then split according to this paragraph 4.

4.4 Payment to Collaborator by Publisher of all net proceeds will be made within fifteen (15) business days after the end of the calendar month in which payments from third parties are received.

1. **OWNERSHIP OF THE WORK; COPYRIGHT:** Collaborator hereby assigns to Publisher the sole and exclusive copyright ownership throughout the world and in perpetuity

of all rights, title of every kind and nature in the Work and in any other material that Collaborator may create in connection with or as part of the Work (including without limitation copyright and the right to create derivative works based on the Work), and waives any moral rights in and to the Work. Included in the rights hereunder shall be right by Publisher to exploit the Work and the Series and all the incidents and characters included therein, using any and all media, whether now known or later created, in all territories, in perpetuity.

1. **WARRANTIES, REPRESENTATIONS, INDEMNITIES:** Collaborator represents and warrants that: Collaborator is free to enter into this agreement; that all rights, including the copyrights, to all the Work created by or for Collaborator by Collaborator or outside sources engaged by Collaborator have been assigned in writing by these outside sources to Collaborator; all contributions to the Work are original or all necessary permissions and releases have been obtained and paid for by Collaborator; and no intellectual property rights have been infringed upon or other laws violated. Collaborator agrees to indemnify Publisher for any loss, liability or expense resulting from the actual breach of these warranties.
2. **NO INJUNCTIVE RELIEF:** Collaborator hereby agrees that during any dispute Collaborator

shall be limited to recover only monetary damages and hereby waives all rights to sue in courts of equity or for injunctive relief.

3. **AUTHORSHIP CREDIT:** Authorship credit(s) for books included in the Work shall be accorded as set forth in Attachment A. Future books not included in Attachment A will require Collaborator's written agreement prior to use of Collaborator's name as author.

1. **CONFIDENTIAL INFORMATION**: Collaborator acknowledges and agrees that all information related to the production of the Work, including without limitation, Collaborator's involvement in the production of the Work, all content, writings, Work product, notes and diagrams ("Confidential Information"), is of great value to Publisher. Accordingly, Collaborator agrees not to divulge to anyone, either during or after the term of this Agreement, any Confidential Information obtained or developed by Collaborator while performing the Work and upon expiration or termination of this Agreement, will deliver to Publisher all documents, papers, drawings, tabulations, reports, audio tapes, video tapes and similar documentation and recording devices which are furnished to or produced by Collaborator pursuant to this Agreement. Upon the expiration or termination of this Agreement, Collaborator agrees to make no further use of any Confidential

Information. Collaborator may only disclose Confidential Information to third parties upon the express written consent of Publisher. The provisions of this Section shall survive the expiration or termination of this Agreement.

1. **RELATIONSHIP OF THE PARTIES:** The parties are independent entities and nothing in this Agreement shall form a partnership, joint venture, employer-employee or similar relationship. It is understood by the parties that this contract is not exclusive and Collaborator may perform similar writing services for others.

1. **WAIVER:** The failure to exercise any right provided in this Agreement shall not be a waiver of prior or subsequent rights.

1. **ASSIGNMENT:** Publisher may assign this agreement, in whole or in part, at any time to any party, as Publisher shall determine in its sole discretion, provided that no assignment shall relieve Publisher of its obligations hereunder unless such assignment shall be to a financially solvent U.S. publisher or to a party that shall acquire all or substantially all of the assets of Publisher. Collaborator may not assign its obligations hereunder to any third party without the written consent of Publisher, Collaborator's obligations being deemed personal; provided that after the

completion of services hereunder, Collaborator may assign the right to receive compensation hereunder to no more than one (1) person or entity.

1. **NOTICES:** All notices which either party shall be required or shall desire to give to the other shall be in writing and shall be given in one of the following ways: (i) by personal delivery, including by established courier service; (ii) by registered, certified, express or priority United States mail, postage prepaid; (iii) by transmittal by any electronic means (such as fax or email) able to be received by the party intended to receive notice (provided that a copy is also delivered by personal delivery or by mail). If so delivered, mailed, or transmitted by electronic means, each such notice shall, except as herein expressly provided, be conclusively deemed to have been given when personally delivered or on the date electronically transmitted, or on the second business day after the date of mailing, as the case may be. The addresses of the parties shall be those of which the other party actually receives written notice and until further notice shall be the following:

If to Publisher:

Publishing company name
Address
Country, Post Code

If to Collaborator:

FIRST NAME, LAST NAME
Address
Country, Post Code

1. **MISCELLANEOUS:** This agreement constitutes the entire agreement between the parties. No modification shall be enforceable except in writing and signed by both parties hereto. This agreement shall be governed by the laws of the United States and the state of ____________ (list jurisdiction of contract) and any dispute arising under this agreement shall be brought before binding arbitration in the state of ____________ (list jurisdiction of contract). The prevailing party to any such dispute shall be awarded reasonable attorneys and arbitration costs.

1. **CRIMES INVOLVING MORAL TURPITUDE:** Collaborator agrees that as a publisher, Publisher is recognized by the general public as a publishing representative of any work Publisher publishes which references Collaborator's original or pen name. Therefore, Publisher reserves the right and Author agrees that Publisher may opt to terminate the Agreement whether there is any charge or criminal conviction of Collaborator of Crimes of Moral Turpitude whether in a private or social context. The term "Crimes involving Moral Turpitude" ("CIMTs") as is used in this Agreement,

refers generally to a range of crimes that are considered to be base, vile, depraved or of sexual immorality. The characterization is based on the "evil intent" or "corrupt mind" of the perpetrator of the crime. While there is no clearly defined list of crimes considered to be CIMTs, they are usually crimes that involve fraud or dishonesty, trustworthiness, sex crimes, those crimes involving serious harm or injury to another or conduct which shocks the public conscience. Upon termination, the rights granted herein to Publisher shall revert to Collaborator, except that termination and reversion shall not deprive Publisher of its right to receive sums which were due or contemplated prior to termination (subject to Publisher's accounting to Collaborator for Collaborator's share thereof).

IN WITNESS WHEREOF, the parties signify their agreement to the foregoing by their signatures below.

PUBLISHER:

By: ______________________________

Name/Title:

Date:________________________

COLLABORATOR:

By; ____________________________

Name/Title:

Date: __________________

ATTACHMENT A

This Attachment A is incorporated to this Individual Collaboration Agreement dated

____________, 20__

Between _________________________ ("Publisher") and

_____________________ ("Collaborator")

The Work: The "Work" and the "Series" as used in the Agreement means the characters and locations currently identified as: _ ___________________________________.

ATTACHMENT B

To Individual Collaboration Agreement dated

____________, 20__

Between __________________________ ("Publisher") and

__________________ ("Collaborator")

Profits on the sale of derivative rights from books covered under this agreement and all works using the Series characters and ideas shall be weighted as follows (to account for marketing and series development costs) and then split according to paragraphs 4 above.

Each book shall count as one unit except for books one and

two. Book one will count as three (unit multiplier) units and book two will count as two (unit multiplier) units.

The total number of units representing the books in Series will based upon a value for each book which is calculated as follows:

Copies Sold x Unit Multiplier = Units

Copies Sold for each book will equal the number of actual copies sold plus the KENP pages read divided by the number of pages for the title (as defined by Amazon). Sales and KENP will be gathered from Book Report, or some other mutually agreed upon publishing reporting service.

As an example, if there are ten titles at the time a derivative right is sold, each book Sold 100 Copies, and books 5-10 were written by Collaborator alone, then weighted value would be calculated as follows:

Title 1 100 X 3 =300
Title 2 100 X 1 =200
Title 3 100 x 1 =100
Title 4 100 x 1 =100
Title 5 100 x 1 =100
Title 6 100 x 1 =100
Title 7 100 x 1 =100
Title 8 100 x 1 =100
Title 9 100 x 1 =100
Title 10 100 x 1 =100
Total of 1,300 units

APPENDIX B-4 - WORK FOR HIRE AGREEMENT

Work for Hire Collaboration Agreement

For books between ____________________ (**Collaborator**) of ____________________ (Address) and ____________________ (**Publisher**) of ____________________ (Address and legal jurisdiction) which are collaborations written in ____________________ (*series title or universe*). This contract is for at least four and as many as eight books in the series. Here are the details:

1) This is work for hire. Collaborator will be paid $0.05 a word for a mostly clean second draft. Collaborator shall be paid 25% of estimated book length up front, 25% at the half-way point, and the remainder when the completed manuscript is delivered. Once the book is published, Collaborator shall receive a quarterly bonus (March, June, September, and December) of 10% of royalties above $5000. For example, after the book has

earned $10,000 total, the bonus would be $500. As work for hire, only the Publisher retains rights in the intellectual property. **Publisher** will provide a monthly accounting of sales and revenue to **Collaborator**. This agreement remains in effect should one of the parties to this contract pre-decease the other. Rights will transfer to heirs or assigns as determined by competent authority. This contract is not transferable.

2) **Publisher** will pay up-front costs for the covers, formal editing, and book formatting (both digital and paperback). None of these costs shall be shared by the **Collaborator**.

3) Collaborator's name will figure prominently on the cover. The inside of the book is going to read something like the information below. The idea is that the ____________________ *series/universe* and characters etc. etc. belong to **Publisher**, who wants protection for all collaborators and understand that by listing collaborators in the front of a book they have the right to question (go to court and have rights) if someone tried to, as an example, sell the movie rights to a book and not include the collaborator in the income payment. As a note, all income for movie rights would be split as defined in paragraph 1).

TITLE (this book) is a work of fiction.
All of the characters, organizations, and events portrayed in this novel are either products of the author's imagination or are used fictitiously. Sometimes both.

This Complete Book is Copyright (c) 2019 by ***Publisher***
Written by **Collaborator** and **Publisher**

4) **Publisher** shall retain sole discretion in the determination of derivative rights from this and all works using the *series name* characters and ideas. Profits from derivative works will be split as defined in paragraph 1).

5) An audiobook version may be produced (unless previous agreed otherwise) within 6 months of book release (often this is within a month - but **Publisher** does not know the future). We will split the cost of the narrator, which will also be taken out of the audio income. **Publisher** will pay the costs for the audiobook up front, and shall recover 100% of those documented costs from initial audiobook proceeds. Following this recovery, any sums over $5000 shall pay 10% bonus to the **Collaborator** on the schedule defined in Para 1) above.

6) No Marketing Expenses are to be apportioned by either party. While it is a smart idea to market our books, we take those expenses on separately. Both **Collaborator** and **Publisher** share in the due diligence to market the book through newsletters (both personal and swapped), social media, and paid ads.

7) This agreement is for the four to eight books in the ____________________ (*series or universe*). The intent is that the manuscripts will be approximately 70,000 words in length and delivered no more than six weeks apart starting as soon as possible. **Publisher** and **Collaborator** will work together to secure a mutually agreeable outline. Collaborator will be compensated for the outline as per paragraph 1). Additionally, Collaborator agrees to maintain a world-building document for continuity's sake, for which collaborator will also be compensated. The books in the ____________________ *universe/series* will be published as soon as **Publisher** determines the best window of opportunity for maximum profitability. This contract will be renegotiated should the series continue beyond eight books.

8) The term of this agreement is for seven (7) years, after which one party may buy out the other at a price to be mutually agreed upon at that time. If that does not happen within 30 days of the 7th anniversary of this agreement, the agreement will renew for an additional seven (7) years, under the same terms.

Agreed and Accepted:

Collaborator: ______________________________

Date: ________________

Publisher: ______________________________

Date: ______________________________

APPENDIX B-5 - ANTHOLOGY AGREEMENT FOR MULTI-AUTHOR SETS

Anthology agreement for multi-author sets

THIS AGREEMENT, made and entered into this ___________ day of _________, 20__, by and between ____________________ **(name of author)**, hereinafter "Author" and ________________, Editor and Publisher, hereinafter "Publisher", and the Short Story, also called "Material" and "Work".

DELIVERABLES

The details are set forth below – this section is provided as a checklist for the Author to follow as an executive summary of the entire agreement.

- By (final delivery date) ____________________________, an original, unpublished Short Story of 6000 to 8000 words in length (in digital form, well-edited, and ready for publication) with a one-liner blurb and short biography with a single link to a preferred landing page

- Short story will be within one of the targeted genre ______________________
- Contributing authors will participate in marketing efforts through engagement in their Newsletters, on Social Media, and other viable platforms/venues that the author uses to promote their works
- Submission will be in Microsoft Word as detailed in Para 1 below

COMMITMENTS

- Short Story remains exclusive to the Anthology for six months from date of publication (target date of _________________________). Actual exclusivity, not to exceed six months (two KDP Select quarters), is at the sole determination of the publisher
- After the exclusion period, the eBook will be unpublished, returning exclusive digital rights to the Author
- Author retains copyright on Author's story at all times
- Anthology will be published exclusively on Amazon unless at the publisher's sole discretion, other digital outlets are deemed more advantageous
- Paperbacks will be published using KDP print and will remain published as paperbacks in perpetuity

- Publisher will pay a royalty advance of ______________. Should royalty share (an equal share to each contributor) exceed _______________/author, then one additional payment will be made the last day of _____________(MMM), __________ (YYYY).
- Publisher is not obligated to accept every story for publication
- If the work is not published by (date) _____________________________, exclusive rights to publication revert immediately as if this contract never existed.
- Cover art and graphics for the anthology will be provided by Publisher

In consideration of the premises and mutual covenants herein contained, the parties agree as follows:

1. CREATION AND DEVELOPMENT OF WORK

Author will create and develop original work as identified below (the "Material") according to the instructions and specifications of the Publisher. Publisher reserves the right to return for revision any and all Material created and developed by Author that does not meet the Publisher's standards for quality and/or is not in keeping with the Publisher's instructions and specifications. Publisher further reserves the right to terminate this Agreement if, in the Publisher's sole discretion, first draft material submitted by Author does not meet the Publisher's standards for quality. Provided this agreement is not terminated, Author is solely responsible for completion of the Material and agrees to make such alterations, additions or modifications at the design stage to the Material as is necessary to complete the Material in accordance with Publisher's standards, instructions, and specifications.

For purposes of this Agreement the term "Material" shall refer to the following item(s):

A short story in one of the Amazon-recognized science fiction genres.

For the purposes of this Anthology, cover art for individual stories will not be accepted or used in publication. The Cover Art will be provided by the Publisher and will be genre-appropriate and impactful for the Anthology.

The original work is to be submitted in the following form (for ease of insertion into the template and reformatting into optimal form – this section is relative, pick your preferred to make your job easier)

- In Microsoft Word without any styles applied (this is important – no styles, don't read into it)
- Title is 14 point Arial bold and centered
- Next line is "By [author's name]" 12 point Arial and centered
- Next line is blank
- All text is left justified and 11 point Arial
- Text within the paragraph is single-spaced
- 6 point spacing will be used between paragraphs.
- If you use chapter headings, they will be 11 point Arial bold, left justified. New chapters will include a blank line preceding

- If you use scene changes, they will be separated three asterisks, left justified (these will become center justified diamonds during the reformatting)

2. DELIVERY TARGETS

Author agrees to submit complete final draft of the Material on or prior to Noon, Eastern Daylight Time, on the date detailed above in the section marked DELIVERABLES. Publisher shall inform Author of whether the story is to be included in the Anthology, no later than one week after final submission date.

Author agrees to provide with the Material a one-liner blurb that will precede the short story within the Anthology, written from the 3rd person point of view.

Author agrees to provide with the Material an approximate one-hundred fifty (150) word biography which should include a link to the Author's preferred landing page.

3. GRANT OF OWNERSHIP AND PUBLISHING RIGHTS

Author assigns to Publisher and Publisher hereby accepts the sole right to first publication of new or previously unpublished Work. Publisher does not have the right to make substantive changes to the Work.

Publisher shall have sole and exclusive rights for six months from the publication date for all purposes, including, without limitation, in connection with the distribution, advertising and exploitation of the work or any part of the work thereof. Publisher is NOT granted the right to make such changes therein and such uses thereof including but not limited to derivative works.

The Author regains the right to publish the material in whole at any time after the exclusion period ends. Publisher shall provide a release letter to Author within five days after the exclusion period ends.

Publisher shall continue to maintain availability of the Anthology in paperback form in perpetuity or for as long as Publisher deems viable. Should Amazon rules change regarding exclusive paperback content to mirror digital rules, Publisher will immediately unpublish the paperback.

The Publisher commissions the Author, who is acting as an independent Author, to develop work with the intent to share rights to such work, within the meaning of the copyright laws of the U.S. or any similar or analogous law or state of any other jurisdiction, with Publisher for exclusive use in The Expanding Universe Anthology, and to produce work that constitutes a commissioned work whose legal owner and author shall hereafter be the Author.

Author retains all copyrights for Author's work and rights to future works with characters and worlds developed within the Author's Material accepted for publication in the Anthology. Author does not have the right to publish works based on the characters or worlds of other Authors published within the Anthology. Author retains moral rights to his/her own work at all times.

4. TERMS OF PAYMENT

Publisher is publishing the Anthology under a profit share of the revenue from sales of the Anthology. Publisher will pay the costs for the cover, advertising, and other Anthology developmental costs. Publisher will share information regarding those costs with the Authors. Once the Publisher recovers those exact costs, all Authors will get an equal share of the remaining profits.

Monthly revenue will be divided by the total number of contributing authors and that will constitute one share. Each Author shall receive a royalty advance of $75 for a story accepted for publication, via PayPal. Distribution of profit shares beyond $75/author following the end of the exclusion period shall be made by the last day of May 2020.

Should paperback royalties accrue to greater than $10/contributing author beyond May 2020, then an additional payment shall be made the month those royalties are paid by Amazon to publisher.

Acceptance of the work shall be at the Publisher's sole discretion. The above agreed-upon consideration compensates Author for all publishing and promotion rights, normal and customary in the industry to the publication of a similar work. This Agreement shall not render Authors an employee, partner, or agent of Publisher for any reason. Publisher shall not be responsible for withholding taxes with respect to Authors' compensation herein. Authors shall have no claim against Publisher for vacation pay, sick leave, retirement, social security, worker's compensation, health or disability benefits, unemployment insurance benefits, or employee benefits of any kind.

5. SAMPLES

Publisher shall provide one digital copy of the finished

Anthology to the Authors via exclusive download from BookFunnel. Paperback copies can be purchased by the Author at cost from KDP Print through the Publisher.

6.EDITORIAL PRIVILEGE

Publisher retains the final editorial privilege on any Material provided to the Publisher from Author hereunder. Author understands that Publisher may alter, add, delete, or otherwise modify the material in any way that it deems, in its sole opinion, necessary to make the material suitable for Publisher's publication needs. It is not the intent of the Publisher to edit Author's work as the work is to be submitted in print ready form. Publisher retains this authority for the sake of consistency of presentation within the Anthology. Author shall be advised of any changes that Publisher proposes.

7.NO CONFLICT AND REPRESENTATION OF ORIGINAL WORK

Author hereby represents and warrants that Author is free to enter into this Agreement and has no other obligations or commitments which would interfere with the full and faithful performance of Author's obligations hereunder. Author further represents and testifies that the work submitted is an original creation, and agrees to indemnify Publisher against actions that rise from prior copyright or copyright violation in the work.

8.CONFIDENTIALITY

Author will not, without the prior written consent of the Publisher, use or disclose to others at any time during or after Author's association with the Publisher (except as may be required in connection with Author's association with the Publisher) any confidential information concerning the Publisher, including, without limitation, information concerning the design or operation of the Publisher's products, advancements or developments in the operation of those products, any technology in use by the Publisher, any data or conclusions obtained by the Publisher, and any profit, cost, customer, or other business information concerning the Publisher. Author will not disclose any confidential information of any person or entity not a party to this Agreement.

The Publisher permits and encourages the Author to discuss the work and to promote the work, both the Anthology and Author's personal Short Story therein. Author also agrees to share announcements regarding the Anthology, in a positive light, to Author's email list, and on other social media platforms that Author uses.

9. GOODWILL.

Author recognizes the value of Goodwill associated with the Material and acknowledges that all copyrights, trademarks, and Goodwill pertaining to the Product shall belong exclusively to the Publisher while the copyright to the original stories will remain the ownership of the Authors. The Publisher acknowledges the Author may publish the material without violation of the product copyrights any time after the contract exclusion period ends. Publisher may copyright and obtain trademarks for all commercial applications of the Product that it may devise, publish, market or produce. Author agrees to represent the Publisher, the Material, and related products in good faith and in the best interest of both parties in all public forums including social media and convention commentaries.

The Author agrees not to inhibit in any way or attempt to limit Publisher's right to advertise, promote, and market the work, including the right to use Author's name and image, as is necessary and usual in the course of business for the sale of the work in all its forms. Such usual promotion includes but is not limited to supplying distributors, retailers, buyers, and media outlets with solicitation information, graphics, advertising, and distribution of promotional material or review copies or trade dress of any publication. The consideration above shall constitute full consideration in relation to any sale or license of any publication of the work in all its forms by the Publisher.

10. WARRANTIES OF AUTHOR.

Author hereby represents, warrants, covenants and agrees, which representations, warranties, covenants and agreements, together with all other representations, warranties, covenants and agreements of Author in this Agreement, shall be true and correct as of the date of this Agreement and shall survive the date of this Agreement, that:

A. Author is the sole and exclusive creator of any new concepts they bring to the development of the Material.

B. The execution and delivery of this Agreement by Author has been duly and validly authorized and approved by all necessary action of Author. This Agreement is a valid and binding obligation of Author, enforceable against Author in accordance with its terms.

11. WARRANTIES OF PUBLISHER.

Publisher hereby represents, warrants, covenants and agrees, which representations, warranties, covenants and agreements, together with all other representations, warranties, covenants and agreements of Author in this Agreement, shall be true and correct as of the date of this Agreement and shall survive the date of this Agreement, that:

A. Publisher is duly organized, validly existing and in good standing under the laws of the State of _______________ (list jurisdiction of contract).

B. The execution and delivery of this Agreement by Publisher has been duly and validly authorized and approved by all necessary action of Publisher. This Agreement is a valid and binding obligation of Publisher, enforceable against it in accordance with its terms.

12. AUTHOR'S CREDITS.

The Publisher agrees to acknowledge, in a conspicuous place, in conspicuous type, in the published version of the Material, Author's contribution to the development of the published commercial product.

Publisher will properly credit Authors as such in any work published by Publisher; however, no liability shall arise by a failure or mistake to do so, although Publisher agrees to make a good faith effort to correct any mistake or lack of attribution in subsequent printings and by correct attribution on Publisher's website. The Publisher will include a copyright notice for the Work in the name of the Authors in the Anthology.

1. INDEMNIFICATION

The Publisher agrees to defend and indemnify Author against any claims, demands, or lawsuits arising out of any finally sustained defamation or finally sustained infringement of any statutory copyright, common law right, right of privacy, or proprietary right of any sort that may occur as a result of publication of any material that is added to the Work by Publisher in the course of developing the Work, including all costs and attorneys' fees associated with such defense and with the enforcement of the duty to defend and indemnify. Authors shall hold the Publisher, its directors, owners, employees, licensees, successors, assigns and agents of the foregoing, harmless and against all claims, liabilities, damages, costs and attorney's fees arising from performance of the Author's duties within the course and scope of this Agreement, or arising outside the course and scope of this Agreement.

14. MISCELLANEOUS.

A. This agreement supersedes and replaces all previous agreements between the two parties concerning the Material and sets forth the complete and only understanding of the Parties and cannot be changed orally.

B. This Agreement shall be binding upon and inure to the benefit of the parties hereto, and their heirs, personal representatives, successors and assigns. The rights of the Publisher hereunder may NOT be assigned to a third party without the consent of Author.

C. The terms of this Agreement shall be construed according to the laws of the State of ____________________ (list jurisdiction of contract).

D. This Agreement may be executed in one or more

counterparts, each of which when so executed shall be an original, but all of which together shall constitute one agreement. Digital copies of the signed agreement are acceptable.

E. If any of the provisions of this Agreement or the application thereof shall be invalid or unenforceable to any extent, it is the intention of the parties that the remainder of this Agreement and the application of such provision to other persons or circumstances shall not be affected thereby and shall be enforced to the greatest extent permitted by law. It is also the intention of the parties that in lieu of each such clause or provision of this Agreement that is illegal, invalid, or unenforceable, there be added as a part of this Agreement a clause or provision as similar in terms to such illegal, invalid or unenforceable clause or provision as may be possible and be legal, valid, and enforceable.

F. Except as otherwise provided herein, time is of the essence.

G. Author agrees to make, execute and deliver any additional documents that may be necessary to carry out this Agreement.

IN WITNESS WHEREOF, the parties hereto have executed this Agreement as of the day and year first above written.

Author: ______________________________ **Date: (M)**___________**/ (D)**_______**/ 20**___

Signature: ____________________________

Author's Preferred Published Name: ____

THE PUBLISHER: Name & Address _______________________________________

By: Signature _____________________________________

If you liked this book, please give it a little love and leave a review. My wheelhouse is Science Fiction, but I have enough experience so the non-fiction makes sense, and hopefully helps you out. If you like this, join the 20Booksto50k® Facebook group as that's where all these conversations and explanations take place. Michael Anderle and I even have a few videos on a wide variety of self-publishing topics. So, you don't need to join my newsletter as I'm not going to promote non-fiction there. But if you like Science Fiction...

You can join my mailing list by dropping by my website www.craigmartelle.com or if you have any comments, shoot me a note at craig@craigmartelle.com. I am always happy to hear from people who've read my work. I try to answer every email I receive.

You can also follow me on the various social media pages that I frequent.

Amazon – www.amazon.com/author/craigmartelle

Facebook – www.faceBook.com/authorcraigmartelle

My web page – www.craigmartelle.com

Twitter – www.twitter.com/rick_banik

AUTHOR NOTES

I am the blue-collar author. I have a law degree, but that doesn't matter, not when it comes to writing. What matters is the willingness to work hard at this thing called self-publishing. I've worked harder, not smarter, on a number of things. I've been fairly successful, but I have much more to learn. In this volume, I'm trying to put some of that good law school knowledge to work for you, as well as the life lessons learned through dozens of collaborations.

Part of what helps me learn is trying to help others. That's what this book is all about. I am sharing what I've done, and I've made many mistakes, some more costly than others. I want to help you avoid those mistakes while also telling you that you aren't alone.

The biggest thank you of all goes to Michael Anderle. He has become a good friend where the business side of stuff is just a footnote to our conversations on life. We've made a difference in people's lives, helped them to help themselves to improve their lots. It's a great feeling that we share. And then of course, to a couple of the contracts that Michael graciously offered as samples in the appendices.

Shout out to my friend Joe Solari who provided some good input regarding the business section. Check out his business books. He knows what he's talking about. I also referred to a collaboration book by Rhett Bruno and Steve Beaulieu and the book by Kevin J. Anderson and Rebecca Moesta. Those are each good books in their own right, regarding the trials and tribulations, victories and failures of collaborating. And most importantly, they talk about what it takes to succeed. I preached about that a fair bit in this volume. Like a marriage. Don't jump in before you've had your first date.

I'm a fan of people doing what they say they'll do. That is the only way you earn trust. Commit to something and do it. Keep your promises. I refer to that a lot in this book, too. Don't promise something if you aren't sure you can deliver. Everyone will be happier. Wishful thinking is great for your motivation but bad for business. A realistic attitude and hard-work is what wins at life. Not everyone has a breakout winner. I don't, but I keep telling better and better stories. I know that big one is coming. I'll keep working toward it.

And there's no reason you can't have a big winner too. Work hard at the right things. Partner with people who will make you better.

Shout out to the review crew! What a great bunch of people.

- Martha Carr (my big sister from a different mister)
- Nora Phoenix

- Crista Crown
- Fatima Al
- Bradley Charbonneau
- Jenn Mitchell
- Brian King

Thank you all. You helped make this book better through your valuable input. The indies who pick up this volume will benefit. I hope we've answered most, if not all, of your questions. Write and publish. There's never been a better time to be a self-published author.

Peace, fellow humans

Craig Martelle

Made in the USA
San Bernardino,
CA